"This book is a must read! Kevin is one of few sages who walks his talk, willing to share both his successes and failures because his heart for others far outweighs any ego or sense of self-importance. Kevin shares real-life stories that not only inspire but also give us the practical tools and frameworks necessary to truly succeed in both life and business. Learn from one of the best, and enjoy (like I did) the incredible wisdom shared within this book."

—**Brandon Schaefer,** author of *Build a Better Life,*
founder of Five Capitals and Legacy Stone

"We all have experiences in life that either work or don't work. Taking time to reflect on these experiences is the best way for us to learn—except when someone like Kevin Rains reflects on *his* experiences, saving us a lot of time and heartache. Kevin offers a wealth of knowledge to help us make better choices. This book is genius!"

—**Mary Miller,** author of *Changing Directions,*
CEO and owner of JANCOA

"Kevin has inspired so many business leaders with his relentless pursuit of purpose and meaning in all aspects of his life. This book will show you how to lead so your business, employees, and you can thrive. Kevin teaches you how to build an amazing company without losing yourself in the process. And he shows you how to stay connected to the sacred purpose of your work."

—**James Lenhoff,** author of *Living a Rich Life*, podcaster,
and cofounder of Wealthquest

"*Profits and Purpose* nails the essence of leadership in just fifteen words: 'Leaders make people happy or drive them to perform. Those who can do both, win.' Kevin Rains found a way to win as he scaled his business over 40X in eighteen years and candidly takes us behind the scenes to learn from the journey. I felt inspired by his honesty, grateful for his vulnerability in sharing his biggest mistakes, and better equipped as he broke down the process he synthesized along the way.

If you want to lead a profitable company, deeply care about the impact your business exerts on your employees and customers, and highly value leaving a legacy that outlives you, buy this book today."

—**Tom Blaylock,** co-author of *Marriage on Mission*, executive leadership coach, and director of training at Legacy Stone

PROFITS *and* PURPOSE

The Christian Entrepreneur's Guide to Growing a Business and Leaving a Legacy

Kevin Rains

Copyright © 2024 Kevin Rains

All rights reserved.

Published by Legacy Press

ISBN: 979-8-9910493-2-0 (hardcover)
ISBN: 979-8-9910493-0-6 (paperback)
ISBN: 979-8-9910493-1-3 (eBook)

Scripture quotations marked NLT are from the Holy Bible, New Living Translation. Copyright © 1996, 2004, 2015 by Tyndale House Foundation.

Scripture quotations marked NIV are taken from the Holy Bible, New International Version®, NIV®. Copyright © 1973, 1978, 1984, 2011 by Biblica, Inc.™

Scripture quotes marked NKJV are taken from the New King James Version ®. Copyright © 1982 by Thomas Nelson.

Printed in the United States of America

For Gary Rains, my dad.

The one who through hard work and a deep faith raised our family from poverty to prosperity, changing the trajectory of our family lineage forever.

"There truly is no division between sacred and secular except what we have created. And that is why the division of the legitimate roles and functions of human life into the sacred and secular does incalculable damage to our individual lives and the cause of Christ. Holy people must stop going into 'church work' as their natural course of action and take up holy orders in farming, industry, law, education, banking, and journalism with the same zeal previously given to evangelism or to pastoral and missionary work."

—Dallas Willard

"To use gifts less than well is to dishonor them and their Giver. There is no material or subject in Creation that in using, we are excused from using well; there is no work in which we are excused from being able and responsible artists."

—Wendell Berry

"Business is a vocation, and a noble vocation, provided that those engaged in it see themselves challenged by a greater meaning in life; this will enable them truly to serve the common good by striving to increase the goods of this world and to make them more accessible to all."

—Pope Francis

CONTENTS

Introduction: *A Pastor's Pivot* 1

1. You: *How to Become a Virtuous Virtuoso* . . . 11
2. Caring for Yourself: *Harmonizing Work and Wellness*. 25
3. Creation: *Turning Vision into Reality* 37
4. Chaos: *How to Grow Your Business and Work through Your Growing Pains*. 53
5. Controls: *Practices to Build Momentum in Your Business* 79
6. Prosperity: *Owning an Asset, Not a Job* . . . 101
7. Legacy: *Outliving Your Earthly Days* 113

Conclusion: *Arrival and Beyond* 129
Acknowledgments 133
Free Bonuses. 134
Appendix: *My Three Biggest Business Mistakes*. 135
Notes 145

Introduction
A PASTOR'S PIVOT

FOR YEARS I viewed my move into business as a demotion. As a child I wanted to be a missionary, and as I grew this desire morphed into a passion for local ministry. Eventually I got a doctorate in ministry and became a pastor. As far as I was concerned, I had arrived.

As a pastor I preached passionately that everyone has a calling. I made it clear being a pastor is not more important than being a shoe salesperson, a plumber, or a customer service rep. Still, I never believed this applied to me. I was a pastor, and I couldn't imagine anything more meaningful.

But after fifteen years of fulltime ministry, I needed to supplement my income. I went back to work in the family business of auto body repair, working for my dad. Eventually my dad helped me launch my own shop in the same neighborhood where I was pastoring.

I remember the tension I felt as my business began to grow. I was angry! I didn't want it to grow, or at least not as much as my church! I wanted to see fruit from my ministry, not profits from my business. It seemed all out of proportion. A little work in my business, and it would grow effortlessly.

The same effort in my church, and very little fruit. But I was called to ministry! This didn't make any sense.

Was I being demoted? Was I letting God down? Was God kicking me off the team? Was I destined to "ride the bench"?

I came to realize, though not accept, I was an "okay" pastor but a good entrepreneur. I even had a close friend at the time tell me, "With a lot of effort and many years of experience, you will be a good pastor. But you have a shot at being a great entrepreneur." Not what I wanted to hear!

I wanted my business to give me just enough money to live, so I could be about my *real* work, my calling, as a pastor. I used to joke that I worked in business to support my "ministry habit." Not having great fruit from my ministry efforts just confirmed that I was "suffering for Jesus." That must be worth some spiritual bonus points, right?

The Doctor Will See You Now

Then I met a doctor who profoundly challenged these assumptions and reoriented my worldview entirely. He lived sometime in the early AD 300s, which means this doctor and I are separated by almost 1,700 years. He lived at the same time as Saint Anthony, the OG desert monk.

Anthony, long before he was "Saint Anthony," responded to Christ's call to the rich young ruler: "Go sell all you have and follow me" (see Mark 10:17–21; Luke 18:18–22). Anthony, hearing this as his personal calling, gave away his large family inheritance. Then for decades he lived a life of solitude and prayer in the Egyptian desert.

Over time others heard about Anthony and followed him into the desert. These men and women who went to the desert were like rock stars in the church. Everyone wanted to meet them or be prayed for by them. They were called "God's athletes." Think Michael Jordan or Tiger Woods, only spiritually. God's very own special forces. The Navy SEALs of faith. Hoo-rah! In most people's eyes, they were a special class of Christian. Respected. Revered. Most considered them the gold standard of what it meant to be a follower of Jesus.

But were they?

On a pilgrimage to Ireland and Scotland I had the oddest experience of receiving God's guidance via books. I found books along my route that really seemed to speak to me. Directly. It was weird. One book would lead me to the next. A book about monastic life in an Irish church library referred to another book on silent prayer. Then I "just happened" to find that exact book in a Scottish bookstore. This occurred over and over. It was like God had me on a scavenger hunt. And at the end of this hunt was the following paragraph:

"It was revealed to Abba Anthony in his desert that there was one who was his equal in the city. He was a doctor by profession and whatever he had beyond his needs he gave to the poor, and every day he sang the Sanctus with the angels."

Whoa! Hold on. You mean there was someone out in the real world, living in a depraved city, being a doctor, managing a business who lived a prayerful and generous life, and he was St Anthony's (gulp!) *equal*?

Yep.

In another story Anthony asks God to show him someone in the city who "is able to reach the same spiritual level as a monk." God directs him to a shoemaker.

These were mind benders for me, forever changing the way I viewed my calling. They revealed to me I can be a prayerful and generous entrepreneur and be really, really close to God. All I ever wanted was to be close to God, which I assumed meant serving him in fulltime ministry. Somehow those two things got woven together. Closer to God + serving him =

fulltime ministry. These stories about the doctor and the shoemaker told me I had it all wrong. It rocked me then. It rocks me now.

It also unlocked me. It unlocked the idea that I could lead an ordinary life as business owner, husband, and father and somehow become equal to one of the greatest saints of all time. Not that I think I've done that, but the possibility excites me. It gives me hope that I can lead an ordinary life and still be extraordinarily close to God and in service to him.

The Story of My Business

Hi, I'm Kevin. May I share a few things about myself so that you can see if we're a good fit? At the risk of sounding prideful, I want to share some of my accomplishments so you will know I'm a competent guide. But don't worry, throughout this book I will be sharing plenty of my mistakes. Want to know my biggest ones? See the appendix. I share them not because I want to balance the scales but because I want to save you a lot of time, money, and heartbreak!

- I am a practicing Christian. I say this because the vast majority of my learning and growth over the past eighteen years has been in the context of trying to live out my faith in the marketplace. Note the words "practicing" and "trying." I have not arrived. But I have made progress.
- I married my college sweetheart, Tracy, thirty years ago. We have three adult children and two grandchildren. I was in the middle of raising young children into their teen and young adult years while building a business. Not surprisingly, that was hard. There's never an easy or perfect time to launch or scale a business.

- I learned how to scale a business from something small to a regional presence—from one location to five, from $250 thousand annually to north of $12 million.
- I have a doctorate degree in leadership development. I know from study and practical experience how to develop leadership skills in others and bring out their latent talents and unique abilities.
- I had a successful exit (selling the business) that allowed me to work on legacy goals like this book as well as some new family enterprises with my children.
- I paid a lot of money on training and coaches and learned from many of the best, collecting tools and concepts along the way that I now can share with you.
- I am a certified executive coach with the Five Capitals coaching network. I'm also a trained Implementer of EOS (Entrepreneurial Operating System).
- In short, I learned from books and in the trenches everything I could about running a business—from finance and marketing to acquisitions and start-ups, from partnerships to HR to strategy and vision and culture. Building and scaling a business is not a theoretical exercise or academic pursuit for me. I studied hard along the way, testing everything I learned in my actual live-or-die business.

Scaling Profits and Purpose

Not everyone will relate to my story. Maybe you weren't in ministry for the first part of your career. Maybe you don't have a problem feeling called to the marketplace. I get that. But what is nearly universal for all Christian entrepreneurs is this: We want to deepen our purpose *and* scale our profits.

We know that with more profit comes more opportunity, more generosity, more time to do what matters most.

When I started my business in 2003, I was clueless. I didn't know what I didn't know. I didn't even know where to begin. But everything I learned from those clueless first years to successfully exiting eighteen years later is contained in this book.

As you grasp and then apply the key ideas in each chapter, you will have a framework for tackling any challenge at whatever stage you find yourself. You will be able to move from launch to legacy. You'll be able to scale both profits and purpose without sacrificing one for the other.

The Framework

Here's the framework in a nutshell.

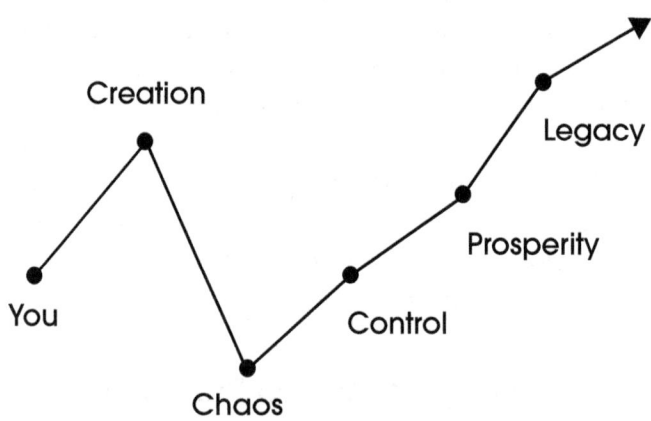

The Profits and Purpose Framework

Businesses go through very predictable life stages. And one builds on the one that precedes it. Once you master the ability to go from one stage to the next, you can scale. I will help you. I will give you tools to make these leaps with confidence.

It will take hard work, and no one can do it for you. But I'm also confident that you really can do this. I've done it. I'll show you how. I will also warn you of the pitfalls and be honest about my shortcomings and regrets so you can learn from me.

The framework starts with you. No matter what your title is—founder, owner, CEO, Grand Poohbah—it doesn't matter. What matters is that you are the prime mover, the biggest influencer in your organization. But before you can influence others, you have to be influenced. And who you are matters more than anything. Who you are determines how effective you will be and how long your legacy will last. The overall outcome of your life and business depends on who you are.

Jesus never told anyone to lead others. But he did tell almost everyone to follow him and to help others follow him. To lead, we must first be followers and learners. Character matters. Being aware of your strengths and limitations matters. Caring for yourself matters. We will discuss all of these.

From the foundation of you and your own self-care, we move next into the first of the five stages in my framework: creation. This is a wondrous stage where we get starry-eyed about the possibilities. This is the dreaming stage, where visionaries thrive. It's a time of naive optimism—as it should be. This is not the time to be realistic, measured, calculated, but rather a time to let your mind and heart soar, to dream of all the things your fledgling enterprise might become.

In this stage we really don't know what we don't know. And that is exactly what propels us into entrepreneurship. If we knew all the challenges and heartbreak that was ahead, we might give up before we even start. This is like the dating phase of a relationship where the partner is viewed as absolutely perfect. Nothing about them annoys us. They can do no wrong, and the future with all its unlimited possibilities is bright as a cloudless day. In addition to dreaming, it's important to get some specific things done at this stage, and in chapter 2 we'll cover them.

The second stage is the reality check. It's the chaos stage. It's where things feel like they are coming unglued. This is where you will feel the most confused, disoriented, and lost. The chaos stage tests your commitment and ability to persevere. If you can clear this stage, things can get fun. And profitable. In this stage you start to realize all the things you don't know.

For me, this was when I realized I couldn't be an accountant, a general manager, head of sales, and the chief operating officer. It was just too many roles. On top of that I was clueless about what most of these roles did and how they did it. I needed help. But I couldn't really afford the help I needed. This felt insurmountable. It wasn't. I made it. And you can make it out of this stage too. Surprisingly, the answer is more simplicity, which we get to in chapter 3.

The third stage is where you gain control. You realize the power of processes, systems, and strategic hiring. You learn that the simplest of tools—the checklist—can be your best friend! Checklists protect and serve us. It's easy to overlook their power, but surgeons and pilots never do! Don't miss that. The people whose jobs involve life and death use checklists! Your business likely isn't life-or-death, but checklists can make or break your success. Chapter 4 is where we'll discuss all this and more.

In chapter 5 we'll dive into the fourth stage, which is where things get really fun: prosperity! This is where your business can run mostly without you. It's where you get to reap the rewards of setting everything up for success and having the right people in the right roles. This is when the business requires the least effort from you of all the stages and makes you the most money.

Lastly, we all want to end up with a legacy that outlives us. This is when the asset we built will bless others in your family and in the wider world. You get to be generous. And whether you sell the business, pass it to a family member, or just let it run on its own, you will be focused on causes and relationships outside your business. You will be leaning most heavily into your *why*, your purpose. And you'll be preparing to leave something behind that will outlive you, hopefully for many generations to come.

If you want to leave a legacy, the good news is you can start right now. Even though legacy is the last stage, it begins now, wherever you are in your personal and professional life. For example, we don't wait to invest in our families until after we have become successful in business. We are always planting seeds for legacy, even in the early stages of a business.

A Caveat

The stages and steps in this book are laid out sequentially. And for the most part this will be the sequence for most of us, most of the time. However, we all know life is not that neat, tidy, and sequential! It's often curly! For example, you need visionary energy from stage one throughout the growth of your business. You may well see sparks of prosperity in the chaos stage. And as I mentioned, legacy runs through all of them like a thread from beginning to end.

From Launch to Legacy

One of my mentors, Michael Hyatt, teaches how we can overcome limiting beliefs. If we catch ourselves expressing a limiting belief, all we need to do is add the word "unless" to the end of the sentence and fill in some options.

Here's a common limiting belief: Business is hard and confusing.

Now let's add "unless." After eighteen years of starting and scaling a business, here's how I would finish it: Business is hard and confusing... *unless* you have an experienced guide who can help you and a framework for understanding where you are and how to get to the next stage. This book is my best attempt to be your guide and to offer you that framework.

Can you build a thriving business that automatically throws off cash with minimal involvement from you once it's built? Can this business serve other goals in your life, a higher purpose both inside and outside the enterprise? Can you scale your values so that everyone is aligned around your purposes and best practices? Can you build a business that will help you leave a meaningful legacy, whether your kids take it over or not? Can you build a business that integrates your faith life without slapping Jesus stickers on everything? In short, can you scale your business all while gaining deeper purpose, better cash flow, and more freedom? Yes, yes, and yes! This book will show you how.

Let's begin.

Access Your Bonuses!

When you bought this book, you also unlocked a package of bonuses designed to help you thrive as a leader and business owner. These bonuses include a list of recommended books, a retreat guide, and a guide on becoming an authoritative yet gentle leader.

Access them all for free here: **www.rainslegacy.co**

1

YOU

How to Become a Virtuous Virtuoso

JUST AS ALL OF CREATION starts with the Creator, your business starts with you. In this chapter, we'll dive into the significance of virtue, self-awareness, and clarity of your goals. Grasping these concepts is key to thriving in business.

Virtue as a Key to Success

Imagine for a moment that your business thrives beyond your wildest dreams, raking in substantial profits, as I truly hope it does! Does this success create a moral dilemma?

The real issue isn't money itself, but our hearts. Virtue is attainable whether we're financially prosperous or not. It's the pursuit of virtue that matters, guiding us through both financial gain and loss. For the Christian entrepreneur aiming to leave a lasting legacy, remember: People may forget your actions or words, but they'll always remember your character.

Take the virtue of integrity, for example. Without it, we risk losing what's most important in our lives. Consider the consequences of an affair—a severe lapse in integrity that often leads to lost relationships, diminished time with children, and material losses in court settlements. This is an example of the direct link between a lack of virtue and significant relational and financial loss.

I'm reminded of Warren Buffett's sage hiring advice: "We look for three things when we hire people. We look for intelligence, we look for initiative or energy, and we look for integrity. And if they don't have the latter, the first two will kill you, because if you're going to get someone without integrity, you want them lazy and dumb." Warren Buffett, arguably the most successful businessman of all time, knows the importance of integrity!

Importantly, Buffet's emphasis on integrity isn't just crucial for individual success; it's a cornerstone for building a thriving business culture.

Virtue, contrary to what many may think, is not a dull slavish adherence to God's commands. Virtue is the most fulfilling way to live and to conduct business. It's good for the soul, and it's good for profits too!

The Culture Factor

This brings us to the heart of the matter: culture. Who you are as a leader gets amplified in your business's culture and ultimately in its reputation.

A business with a strong culture can grow and remain true to itself and its values without the leader having to always be there to provide guidance on every little decision. In my industry, a strong shop culture is what can carry a shop's good reputation far and wide.

And culture, for better or worse, is rooted in the character of the business owner and managers.

Each business has a way of accomplishing core tasks such as finances, operations, or human resources. And how you build culture affects all of them. Culture can be implemented haphazardly or well. It can be strong or weak, clearly defined or just a set of assumptions in the manager or owner's head. But every business has a culture. My goal is for you to have a good one that is intentionally built and nurtured and able to consistently guide your business toward health and high performance.

Culture begins at the top. Whether it's your immediate family or your business, sports team or the PTA, all groups have a way of operating that reflects the leader. If you are a manager, leader, or owner, you are responsible for the culture and it will reflect you—the good and the not so good! And keep in mind that your character matters. How you treat others will eventually come to light. More importantly, your organization will increasingly reflect who you are.

Many companies have a list of core values that guide their operations. One of the most famous companies of all time had these values posted in their lobby: "Integrity. Communication. Respect. Excellence." Care to guess which company that was? The company was Enron, whose leaders all went to jail and the company itself went bankrupt because of fraud.

What is the link between culture and character of leadership?

Aristotle said, "We are what we repeatedly do." In other words, we get what we tolerate! And what we tolerate becomes our default culture!

A Cautionary Tale

Let me tell you about Joey Buttafuoco, who represents a cautionary tale from the auto body industry. If you're under forty you may have never heard of Joey, as his star faded as quickly as it ascended, though he tried to keep himself in the spotlight for as long as possible. His list of moral failures and their consequences is impressive:

1. Joey had an affair with Amy Fisher, a sixteen-year-old customer he met at his shop.
2. He was convicted of statutory rape and did four months in jail.
3. Amy Fisher shot his wife in the face on the porch of their home. (Fortunately, Mary Jo Buttafuoco survived the shooting.)
4. After that incident, Joey Buttafuoco was indicted on nineteen counts of statutory rape, sodomy, and endangering the welfare of a child, to all of which he eventually pled guilty.
5. After this, the Buttafuocos remained married for a time, moved to California, then divorced in 2003.
6. In 1995, he pled no contest to solicitation of a prostitute.
7. In 2004, he pled guilty to insurance fraud and did another year in jail plus five years probation. He is no longer allowed to work in the auto body industry in the state of California for the rest of his life.
8. Joey became the punchline of many of David Letterman's jokes in his last year of hosting *Late Night with David Letterman*.
9. He was parodied in many *Saturday Night Live* sketches.

If one were to compile a list of all the things that might be done to discredit and embarrass a business, even an industry, this list hits the nail on the head!

And in the current climate, both in politics and Hollywood,

with woman after woman—and some men as well—coming forward to accuse politicians and entertainment stars of inappropriate use of their status, wealth, or power to gain sexual favor, we are starting to see how much character matters.

What we need are more leaders, managers, and owners who have integrity. Don't be like Joey!

Virtuous Virtuoso

I remember being at my first Strategic Coach session. Strategic Coach is a business that provides business coaching. Every quarter I met with about twenty-five entrepreneurs to learn tools to help us grow our businesses all while finding more freedom. Ross, the facilitator of my group, started the first session by having each of us introduce ourselves in the following way:

"I am an entrepreneur with a unique ability to _____."

It was a brilliant way to start the meeting as well as our journey with Strategic Coach because it reinforced what we had in common—we were all entrepreneurs—yet we were all unique and had special abilities.

I remember introducing myself: "Hi, I'm Kevin. I'm an entrepreneur with a unique ability to grow auto body shops." Something clicked in my brain at that point. I had a new understanding of who I was. I was not just an auto body shop owner. I was someone who had the ability to grow auto body shops.

In the years since then, I eventually owned five auto body shops and now help others grow their businesses through coaching, writing, and speaking. It became a bit of a self-fulfilling prophecy. Or perhaps it just helped me realize who

I already was. Regardless, it was a clarifying and helpful moment.

You are great at something. A big part of your life's work is to become a virtuoso of your own unique gifting. How would you introduce yourself if you were in the room that day? Try filling in the blanks below.

> Hi! I'm _____. I am an entrepreneur with a unique ability to _____.
> Send me an email and let me know.
> My email address is kevin@rainslegacy.co
> I'd love to hear from you!

As Socrates is thought to have said, "Know thyself." Your first step to a prosperous future is discovering more about who you are, how you're wired, and what you uniquely offer the world.

YOU are the brand.

You may not be aware yet of what makes you unique, but you are already great at something. Discovering this unique ability, this strength that is distinctly yours, is a large part of your life's work. And once discovered and named, you can then become responsible for it and nurture and refine it. Eventually you'll become a one-of-a-kind virtuoso at your unique ability.

But what if you have trouble figuring out what your unique ability is? Maybe you had difficulty filling in the blanks above. Maybe something immediately came to mind, but you'd like to have it confirmed.

Your friends and family can help here. They have a perspective on you that you can't have. If you really want to know what your thing is, start by asking them what they see. You could say or write something like, "I'm trying to discover what I'm good at. Can you tell me how I have contributed to your life?" You can literally do that right now. Just send out a few emails with that question. What you'll find is that everyone will say something different on the surface, but underlying the feedback will be patterns and themes that are unmistakable.

Right here is where you're probably telling yourself, "I can't ask my friends that question. Its sounds so self-serving." Well, it's not. It's simply one part of the discovery process you'll use to become more useful, more capable of doing what you are uniquely able to do. It will help you contribute to the good of the world. Here's the deal: Once you know what your special strength is, *then* you can consciously put it in service to others. In that light you can think of it this way: It's actually selfish *not* to discover your distinctive gift. We want you to discover it. We need you to.

Irenaeus said, "The glory of God is a person fully alive." Howard Thurman said it this way: "Don't ask yourself what the world needs. Ask yourself what makes you come alive, and go do that, because what the world needs is people who have come alive."

An Ongoing Process

Asking friends and family about your unique gifting is important, but other avenues for discovery can be very helpful. Some of the great tests and tools on the market include the Myers-Briggs Type Indicator (MBTI), the Enneagram personality test, StrengthsFinder, and the Kolbe Strengths Assessment. These are ones I've used and can confidently recommend. Executive coach Dan Sullivan's concept of "unique ability" took me far down the path as well. But honestly, none of these gave me the full picture. They were more like pointers toward what my thing is, and I'm still not 100 percent sure I got it right. I'm still discovering. This is an onion that gets peeled over years, not a fifteen-minute assessment or even a half-day seminar.

For now, just peel a layer at a time. And with each layer, you get closer to discovering your unique strength, you become a little more self-aware. And as you become more self-aware, you become increasingly better able to serve, love, and care for those around you.

The payoff is huge. Great rewards will follow each successive layer. At first it may be just the psychological and self-reinforcing reward of being good at something, so your confidence increases. Then as you peel further down you find that your joy also increases. The rewards seem to get more and more tangible. Soon they'll include things like recognition and even revenue.

Looking in the Mirror

As we begin the journey of discovering our unique gifting, we begin with the process of increasing our self-awareness. For most of my teen years I was told by friends and teachers I had great "leadership potential." Yet I had no idea how to go from "potential leader" to "actual leader." Looking back some twenty-five years later, it turns out the path is not really that big of a mystery.

The biggest contributing factor to making the journey is self-awareness, and a key element is understanding how other people experience us. Once we become aware of how our actions, words, and attitudes move people—for good and bad—we can go to work honing the parts of our leadership that need to improve.

As a young man, I was very headstrong, naive, and lacking in self-awareness. I had plenty of self-assurance and confidence. But I didn't have a clue about how I came across to others or how my actions, attitudes, and words affected the people around me. In short, I was oblivious to what I was leaving in my "wake"—those things we're not aware of that agitate the emotional waters behind us.

Inexperienced leaders have what some leadership development experts call "unconscious incompetence." That is to say, they don't know what they don't know. This especially applies to how their actions and attitudes affect the people who look to them for guidance.

To become a better leader, the next stage everyone must pass through is "conscious incompetence." This is the hardest stage because here you become keenly aware of what you don't know. Here, blissful ignorance ends and you begin to realize you have to acquire new skills, mindsets, and knowledge.

Of course the goal is to get to the point of "unconscious competence," where you just lead naturally by instinct and you don't even have to think about the right course of action; you just know.

I encourage you to pause right now and consider: Where are you on this continuum?

So in addition to exploring our unique gifting, how do we increase self-awareness? The possibilities are endless, but I encourage you to start with three simple steps.

1. *Ask those who work with you how you're doing.*
   Ask them face-to-face if there's anything you do or don't do that helps or hinders them. Ask them how you could become a better leader. Trust me: People around you will have an opinion on this if you ask sincerely with a desire to grow and learn. If you are committed to listening and not trying to justify yourself or explain your actions or manage your reputation, your people will tell you.

2. **Pick a test or two.** The same tests you can use to discover your unique gift can also help you find out how you're wired and give you insights into preferences you may not even know you have. These tests can also help you answer questions about those around you and why they do some of the things they do. For instance, being an introvert, I thought I had to be an extrovert to be a good leader. Turns out, introverts can make great leaders, but they need time to refuel with time alone between engagements. A constant flow of people with little to no time to think wears introverts out. I've learned to take time alone to recharge my inner battery so I can engage better when the time comes.
3. **Look for what bothers you in other people.** When do you tend to get frustrated with others' behaviors? Those irritants are clues to areas we might want to take a look at in ourselves. One of the greatest psychologists ever, Carl Jung, said, "Everything that irritates us about others can lead us to an understanding of ourselves."

Self-awareness is like peeling an onion. You're not going to get it all at once. It takes time. Just begin peeling it one layer at a time. As you gain self-awareness little by little, the aha's will start to pile up. You will be all the better for it, and so will those you lead.

Looking through the Johari Window

Another great tool for building self-awareness is the Johari Window, created by American psychologists Joseph Luft and Harry Ingham. Understanding this is simple, and it will help you cultivate trust and open communication with those around you. The goal is to have open and honest communication in every direction with your team and family.

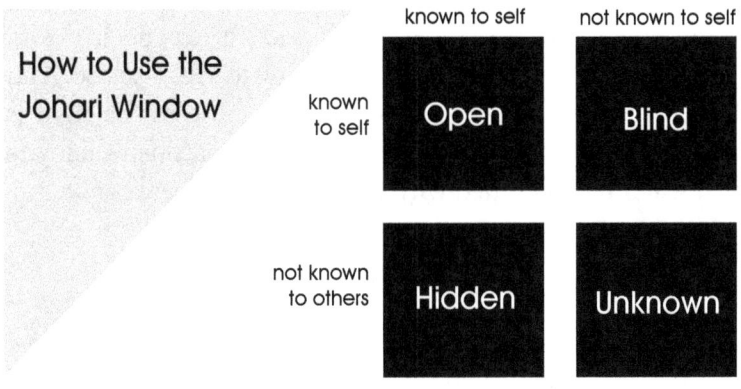

Johari Window

The upper left is called the "Open area." These are things you know about yourself, and your friends, family, and coworkers know them too. These are things like what you like and don't like, what your previous job was, and where you plan to vacation this year.

The upper right corner is the "Blind area." These are things others see in you but you don't see in yourself. An example here may be that you have low self-confidence. You may not see that, but those around you day in and day out can see it.

The bottom left or "Hidden area" includes things you know but you haven't shared with others. Secret dreams or temptations or even challenges that run in your mind but for whatever reason you choose not to reveal to others. This is the area where if you risk vulnerability, you can likely deepen your relationships with others significantly.

Finally, the bottom right is the "Unknown area." These are the things that remain off the radar. You don't know what they are and neither does anyone around you.

To grow and deepen your relationships it's best to keep enlarging the "Open area." To expand the "Open area" to the right, you'll need to ask for feedback. To expand it down, you'll need to decide what you're willing to self-disclose. And to get this moving simultaneously down and to the right is called shared discovery; it only happens via open dialogue and listening combined with honest self-disclosure.

What Do You Want?

Listening to others and their perception of you—there's just no substitute for that. But self-analysis is also important. A great way to deepen your self-analysis is by asking a simple but tough question: What do you want? What do you really, really want?

Think of this in categories—what some call the "Five Capitals." Pull out some paper or a journal and write about half a page in response to each of the following questions:

1. What do you want spiritually? Not just a religious question but what do you want in terms of meaning and higher purpose? Do you feel called to anything? Is there some issue in the world you would like to tackle? Do you ever crave solitude?
2. What do you want relationally? What do you want your family life to look like? How many and what kind of friends would you like to have? What about intimacy with a life partner or spouse? Who are your mentors? Who are you mentoring? Who are your peers? Professionally,

what kind of relationships are you cultivating?
3. What do you want mentally? How are you stretching yourself to learn and grow? What books are you reading or want to read? Are there classes you'd like to take or subjects you'd like to learn about? If you could be an expert on something, an authority, what might that be? Do you want to write?
4. What do you want physically? Do you have an age you'd like to live to? What about your weight or appearance? What kind of diet and exercise appeal to you? What healthy habits are you engaging? Are you getting enough rest, enough sleep? What ailments do you have that you'd like to overcome?
5. What do you want financially? If you didn't have to worry about money, what would you do? What kind of savings or investments would you like to have? What kind of inheritance would you like to leave? To whom? For what? How are you engaging generosity?

Now answer: *What surprised you in this reflection from what surfaced? What are three or four key words that jump out at you as you review this list? How might you summarize this into a sentence or two? Into a few words? Into one word?*

2

CARING FOR YOURSELF
Harmonizing Work and Wellness

WHEN JESUS SUMMARIZED the Law, he said, "Love the Lord your God with all your heart, soul, mind and strength and your neighbor as yourself" (see Mark 12:30–31). It's easy to see this commandment as twofold: Love God, love neighbor. But what about that last little phrase "as yourself"? Was Jesus assuming we would love and care for ourselves? I think so. Loving self is a necessary precursor to loving others.

Steven Covey shares a relevant story in his chapter on the seventh habit in *The 7 Habits of Highly Effective People*. He asks you to imagine coming upon a man in a forest who is laboriously trying to fell a tree. The man tells you he's been at this for hours. "This is hard work," he says. You sensibly suggest taking a break to sharpen the saw, but the man retorts: "I don't have time to sharpen the saw. I'm too busy sawing!"

If we want to do our best work and love well, we need to sharpen our most important tool: ourselves.

Morning Ritual

We are all used to the idea of managing our time, but what about our energy? If we are not bringing energy to work, we will constantly be underperforming and not using our available time well. Here's a practice I recommend: *Develop a morning ritual.*

Lately I've been using the acronym PLAN for my morning ritual: Prayer, Learning, Activate, and eNcourage. Let me explain.

Every morning I start my day with *Prayer*. This involves saying set prayers, reflecting prayerfully on Scripture (I use a practice known as *lectio divina*), and silence.

Next I focus on *Learning*. I read something that nourishes my mind or provokes me to think more deeply or differently about a topic of interest. This reading might be business- or faith-related.

Then I move to *Activate*. This is where I get my body moving. I stretch. I get my heart rate up. A brisk walk, the stationary bike. Something that raises my heart rate.

I end with *eNcourage*. This is where I think about my family and a few close friends and then send them an email or text letting them know they were on my mind. I do my best to encourage them.

Some mornings I have an hour or more for all the above. Other mornings it's just a few minutes. But my goal is to start my day by hitting all those domains. And of course it can also be used at the end of the day.

This little cluster of habits ensures that I'm not just working on things but on myself. It allows me to bring my best efforts to whatever is before me on any given day.

Solitude

Think of all the revelation leaders in the Bible received from experiences in solitude. Moses spent time in the wilderness, alone, before receiving the Ten Commandments.

David spent countless nights alone with only his herd of sheep for companions. As a shepherd he likely walked for days at a time seeking food and water, green pastures of rest for his herd.

Then there's Paul, who spent seven years in Arabia before launching into his world-changing mission to the Gentiles. And of course, no biblical list would be complete without Jesus, who lived a very normal life by all accounts until he was thirty. Then he spent forty days in the wilderness, alone, being tested before he began his ministry.

Intentional rest in solitude is the birthplace of inspiration. In addition to these Bible figures, great leaders throughout history and from around the globe have strategically practiced solitude—Gandhi, Martin Luther King Jr., Winston Churchill, and Abraham Lincoln, just to name a few. They spent significant time in solitude and deep reflection. Solitude is the grist mill for great ideas, rejuvenation, and clarity.

And yes, there is a great paradox here. To accomplish much, we first must rest. To lead others well, we need to be alone.

How to Be Alone

As I was writing this book, I did a search for *Harvard Business Review* articles on solitude and leadership. I had a faint recollection of reading an article years ago about the power of solitude for leadership development. But when I did the search, what caught my attention was the full page of results on "loneliness of leaders."

It's easy to confuse solitude with loneliness, but they are very different. In fact, one of our best modern teachers on the spiritual life, Henri Nouwen, taught that solitude is actually *the cure* for loneliness.

I remember leading a retreat for business owners where one of the participants, a man we'll call Joe, mentioned offhandedly he could not remember a time when he had ever intentionally been alone as an adult. Joe did, however, remember many times in his childhood when he spent a lot of time outdoors, alone, lost in his thoughts and imagination.

He remembered those times being very rejuvenating and life-giving. "But now," he said, "I can't even go to the bathroom without one of my kids banging on the door trying to get my attention." He told me later while we were hiking that he didn't even know how to spend time alone. It was almost as if he wouldn't know what to do if he was alone.

At a certain point in our hike I said, "You go that way and I'll go this way. We'll meet up at the main camp whenever you get back. The very first step toward practicing intentional solitude is simply to be alone with your thoughts. See you in a bit."

I got back to the main camp and waited for him. And waited. And waited. At one point I wondered if I should go and check on him. Eventually he emerged from the woods and back to the main camp. I asked him how it went. "I just found this overhang and sat on a rock for twenty minutes. It was amazing!"

He literally looked different to me after this brief experience of solitude. Here's a man—husband and father—who had not experienced any solitude as an adult. In twenty minutes he got in touch with something he did routinely as a child, and it visibly changed him. He looked younger, lighter, beaming with joy and peace.

> **Free Retreat Guide**
>
> My son, Izaac, created a guide to help you design a retreat for yourself. Download it for free at **www.rainslegacy.co**

Childlike Rejuvenation

I love the word *rejuvenation*! It literally means to be made young again. *Re* is the prefix that means "again." And the Latin word *juvenis* is also the root word for *juvenile*, meaning "young one." How do we rejuvenate?

On the retreats I lead, I encourage everyone to think about what they did in their childhood that made them feel alive. If we can tap into things that made us feel alive when we were young, hopefully we'll find clues to what will make us feel young and fully alive again.

As a child I was outside a lot, typically playing or hiking in the woods. Then it was making trails and jumps and going through the woods fast on my BMX bike. As I got older, I graduated to motorcycles and my trips through the woods got faster and faster. Eventually I got my driver's license and just had to have a convertible! I found a 1969 Olds 442 ragtop and restored it over the summer before my senior year in high school with help from my dad and his team at the shop.

I used to love to take Sunday drives through local parks. I also tried to see how fast it could go. Let's just say I was chased but never caught! In short, what I realized as I looked back on these experiences is that I really like to go fast in nature. When this dawned on me about ten years ago, I immediately bought a motorcycle. I nicknamed it my "two-wheel therapy." It turned out that riding motorcycles makes me feel young again.

How do you experience rejuvenation? What did you do when you were young that made you feel alive? I would love to hear from you! Email me and let me know (Kevin@rainslegacy.co). And if you're looking for some time away, we'd love to have you on one of our retreats (dappledlightadventures.com).

Find a Hobby

Riding motorcycles is now a hobby of mine. Somehow in the hustle of growing a business and the bustle of raising children, I never found time for what seemed like the unnecessary extravagance of hobbies. As I look back on those years, I also see a stressed-out, often angry-for-no-apparent-reason young man who probably needed the outlet a hobby would have provided.

This older and hopefully wiser version of myself seems to have finally embraced the rejuvenating role of hobbies. I discovered I love fishing (or rather catching), golf (yes, I'm horrible, but what a great excuse to be outside!), and riding motorcycles. I embraced all three of these in the past few years in ways that border on the fanatical. And it has been beyond good for me, in both body and soul.

If you don't have any hobbies but would like to nurture some, I have a few tips:

1. Try answering this question: If you could do anything at all and you weren't allowed to give it a deadline and you weren't allowed to receive money for doing it (in other words, you could only do it for fun), what would it be?
2. Try asking people you enjoy hanging out with what they do for fun and see if that provides

any insights. Like right now, send a text to a couple people you admire and ask them.
3. Don't overthink it, and start small. If you think you might enjoy biking, don't go out and buy an expensive bike! Rent a bike for half a day.
4. Look at your dream vacations for clues. Are you more of a mountain or beach person? If mountain and you don't live near them, perhaps you can try hiking in your area. Or if beach consider a scuba lesson!

Stop Working to Get More Done

When we manage our energy, we are able to use our available time more fully. With more energy, the time we have seems to expand and we're able to get more done. In this way, the path to getting more done is often counterintuitive: Stop working, rest deeply, rejuvenate. Then come back to the tasks at hand with renewed energy.

For observant Jewish people this is part of their weekly religious practice as a Saturday Sabbath, when all work stops for twenty-five hours. Culturally these practices have led us to what we call "the weekend," even though it's really two days with one day being the end and the other the start of the new week. Most people get a couple of days off per week and that is a good thing, if at all possible.

A tricky thing about weekends, though, is that it can be easy not to take them as downtime. This is especially true in this digital age where we have great tools that can bind us like chains to a never-ending cycle of work.

Yes, I'm talking about our smartphones. I have a love-hate relationship with mine. On the one hand it is like a Swiss Army knife of digital tools in my pocket at all times. On the other it allows me to be at work 24/7. What if our weeks went to 24/6 or even 24/5? What if we could actually take one or two days off completely every week? The keyword here is *completely*.

I have a friend who talks about days off in archery terms. Days off work are like pulling the bowstring back. The farther you pull the bowstring back, the farther the arrow flies when it is released. The more rest we get, the better we are able to perform at our work. Our rest leads to the arrows of productivity flying much farther.

Rest, Then Work

I remember taking a walk with my friend James on our retreat property. He asked, "Why do some Jews and Christians say the day starts in the evening? That seems so backwards to me!" I had to admit I had never given it that much thought, though I knew it to be true. But if the day starts in the evening, when we normally sleep, the focus is on taking rest. Even our shared origin story in Genesis 1 reinforces this. What did God create on the sixth day? Man and woman. What did he do on the seventh day? Rest. Our first full day as a race was designed to be a day of rest with God.

The more we talked about it, the more I realized maybe it was tied to the idea that most of us, especially in the West, value our work life so much that we perceive our day starts when we start working. We get up and go to work. And that's the start of our day! But is it? In God's economy, is that really when the day starts? Or were the biblical writers really onto something here that expresses more of God's heart? Perhaps God values rest more than work? At a minimum we can say rest comes before work!

How Change Happens

How do we change? I've given you a lot of instruction about virtue, self-awareness, and self-care, but what if you don't like where you are in any of these areas? How do you change?

I'd like to share a method for personal change I've found helpful. While it's not unique to her, I first heard it in this format from Brooke Castillo.

In our lives we have *circumstances, thoughts, feelings, actions,* and *results. Circumstances* are those things in life over which we have no control, such as the weather, politics, and other people. *Thoughts* are what we think about those things that are both within and outside our control. Two people can have a very similar experience but think about it differently. *Feelings* are how we feel about something. *Actions* are how we behave based on our feelings. *Results* are the outcomes of our actions.

These steps are important to understand when we want to make a change. When trying to change, we often fall victim to two mistakes. The first is we try relying on our will power, which doesn't tend to go well. We try to attack change at the level of action. I will eat better. I will sleep more. I will stop smoking. I will . . . there's a lot of "will" in there! We tend to overestimate our will power and self-control.

The second mistake is we assume our feelings are not in our control. That is not true. We do not need to be ruled by our emotions. Our emotions are the direct result of our thoughts, over which we do have control. If we correct our thoughts, we change our feelings. Dallas Willard said our feelings are great servants but horrible masters. They serve us by telling us what we are thinking so that we can adjust our thinking. Feelings are like thermometers, which measure the temperature. Thoughts are thermostats, which set the temperature.

We control our thoughts, which lead to our feelings, which lead to our actions, which drive our results.

Do you want to change? Focus on your thoughts.

A Personal Reflection

Let me share how all of this worked out in my own life.

I had fallen into an unhealthy and unsustainable routine. With the recent acquisition of a new business, my workload seemed to be double or even triple what it was prior. I was learning the hard lesson that I could not be in two places at once. The wake-up call for me came when it started affecting not just me but those I love, my family.

I was coming home exhausted. I had nothing left in the tank to give them when I got home. All I wanted to do was eat dinner and stare at a TV screen or go to bed early. Neither of those fostered a warm home environment. Instead of my wife and children being excited to see me come home, I would get questions like, "Dad, are you okay? You look tired!" And I was. I was not leaving anything in the tank for the ones who matter the most to me.

My circumstances had changed. My thoughts about those changes were putting me in a place of despair. I was scared.

When I realized what was going on in my thinking, I shared it with my business coach and we began unpacking it. He knows me well. Not because he has been my business coach for a long time, but because he has seen it in countless others. I am a classic "type A" personality. Couple that with being an introvert who is often forced into extroverted roles like leadership, sales, and customer service, and voila! I often found myself living in the red, deficit spending emotionally and physically.

With my coach I started to realize I needed first to change

my mindset then develop several new habits that would allow me to avoid getting depleted. The mindset shift that took place was learning to trust others on my team. I also needed to reset how I ended my day. I assumed I needed to end the day in a flurry of extroverted activity. What I realized was that what was best for me, my customers, and my team was to actually end the day with work that was more suited to my energy level at that time. With these subtle mindset shift, sparked by my coach, I was able to turn my attention to new behaviors.

Here are four that we came up with:

- **First**, I needed to be accountable to someone who would check in with me regularly about how I was doing in this area. We agreed that part of our regular coaching call would be a check-in time devoted to him asking me if I was practicing the new routines we agreed on.
- **Second**, I needed some off-ramps toward the end of my day that would allow me to more easily transition from work to home. Typically, I would work right up to the end of the day on things that drained me: delivering cars, interacting with customers, and directing my team. As an introvert, I was going 100 mph on tasks that even extroverts would find challenging!

  For me, it was completely depleting at a critical time. My coach encouraged me to trust my team with these tasks while I would attend to less people-intensive but very important tasks like following up on customer emails and gathering and organizing performance data from all my shops. These were the kinds of tasks that I could do alone, at my desk, quietly and without interruption.

- **Third,** I had a new "coming home" routine. It started by getting home a half hour before dinner so I can unwind. My wife and I agreed that when I got home I would greet her and my kids and then have about thirty minutes to myself to do something that would help me get my mind entirely off the shop. Sometimes I watch a few funny videos (Jimmy Fallon usually does the trick) or catch up with friends on Facebook. I will typically have some music I enjoy playing in the background as well.
- **Fourth,** my coach and I decided I needed one full day per week of not working. This may seem obvious and easy to some, but I find it very difficult to completely disconnect. For example, my shop emails came to my phone. So the temptation to check email on a Sunday was very high. And I usually fooled myself into thinking it really wouldn't affect me. So I would take a peek. If I read an email from a customer with an unmet expectation, however, I would start a dialog in my mind with that customer on why their expectations were wrong, all the extra things we've done for free already, and the written agreement that clearly documents what had been agreed on. Before I knew it, that one little email that took me a minute to check became the focal point for my entire day.

For me, having a real free day is hard. But when I do it, I go into the week rested and much more ready to tackle challenges with a fresh perspective on what really matters.

These mindset shifts led me to experience different feelings, which naturally led to different actions, which changed the results for better—both for me and my family.

3

CREATION

Turning Vision into Reality

GENESIS OPENS, "In the beginning God *created* the heavens and the earth" (my emphasis).

Right from the start, God is revealed as a creator. And that word *creator* can be interpreted in a variety of ways: artist, artisan, builder, maker. It's not much of a stretch to throw the word *entrepreneur* in there too.

We are created in God's image, with an innate desire to make things, invent things, start things. You may be feeling this impulse even now. It's that spark of creativity that leads us to the thrill of beginning something new.

The start-up stage! What a rush! The possibilities are endless. And what a wonderful stage this is. Many refer to it as the honeymoon stage. Of course marriages aren't built on great honeymoons, but they sure are a fun way to launch one!

What Entrepreneurs Do

At times I've heard entrepreneurs praised as gods in our culture. At other times I've heard them vilified as nothing more than greedy exploiters. Neither of these extremes is helpful.

In light of these misconceptions, our first step is to define our terms. According to Merriam-Webster dictionary, an entrepreneur is "one who organizes, manages, and assumes the risks of a business or enterprise." That is a good, basic start. Yet that could apply to almost anything from a lemonade stand to a nonprofit organization to a multinational corporation. And it doesn't really answer the question of what an entrepreneur actually *does*.

Jean-Baptiste Say, a French economist who first coined the word *entrepreneur* in about 1800, sheds some light on what entrepreneurs do. He said, "The entrepreneur shifts economic resources out of an area of lower and into an area of higher productivity and greater yield." So entrepreneurs are those who manage resources in a productive way that benefits themselves and others.

How Christian Entrepreneurs Operate

Now what can make entrepreneurial pursuits distinctly Christian? For that to happen, all efforts need to be in line with Christian understandings and practices. In other words, they must be guided by the mind of Christ, and those involved must practice virtues consistent with the call of Christ:

- humility
- generosity
- care for team members and creation
- prayerful dependence on God and not oneself
- actions that are not rooted in anger or lust
- non-anxious

These are just a few, most of which come from Christ's central teaching in the Sermon on the Mount in Matthew 5–7.

To me, being a Christian entrepreneur has meant launching and leading a group of auto body shops. We grew from one small shop to five. But it's not just *that* we grew, it's how. We fostered a culture of care in our shops.

We cared for our customers through empathy. We cared for our craft by doing high-quality repairs—even the hidden stuff that no one sees after the repair but it makes the repair stronger and safer for the long haul. We cared for the communities we served through generosity. We cared for the earth by using water-based paints that don't compromise the longevity of the finished product but reduce our environmental impact by 97 percent in contrast to solvent-based paints. We cared for our team members by offering them the opportunity to grow and expand in their role through training and development that we paid for.

In short, we strived to love our neighbors, our neighborhoods, and the earth while operating from a Christian lens. We also failed. And repented. This too is also part of being a Christian entrepreneur and probably the best starting point.

Be Like Elon?

I know there are a lot of people who want to be like Elon Musk. He is currently the richest person on the planet. He founded two extremely well-known companies worth billions: Tesla and SpaceX. He is sometimes compared to the fictional Iron Man. He has huge vision and bold ideas and the ability to execute them. He has a very high IQ. Sounds pretty good when we put it like that, right?

Elon has a prodigious output. He gets things—BIG things—done. He has incredible ideas and vision, and he is able to execute, bringing those ideas to reality and eventually to market. I'm sure a lot of people have had ideas about building electric cars for a long time. Yet Elon actually did it. And not just as an inventor but as an entrepreneur. He not only built the most successful electric car to date but also the most recognized brand in that space. And yes, there are big competitors coming after him. And with the amount of money at stake, they will likely invent something superior, but he will always be the one who was first to market. He made his mark. History has been made. And it looks like he will continue to make history with several other projects, most notably SpaceX.

What I do not find compelling, however, is the pace and amount of time he spends working at the expense of his health and family life. Many believe he has been on the verge of a mental breakdown on numerous occasions.

Tim Denning, a popular writer for Medium.com, calls Elon a slave, labeling his work ethic psychopathic. He summarized a *New York Times* interview where Elon welled up with emotions as he shared about his 120-hour work week, the fact that he worked twenty-four hours straight on a recent birthday, that he hasn't had a week off since 2001, and the fact that he rarely goes outside, staying in his factory three to four days at a time. That does not sound healthy or sustainable, at least not for me or anyone I know personally.

Jesus once asked, "What does it profit you if you gain the whole world but lose your own soul?" (see Mark 8:36). And the obvious answer is: Nothing. If we sacrifice our health and our most important relationships on our way to the top, we will have nothing to show for it in the end. Do we really think our spouses, kids, and friends will be grateful for the extra money we leave behind or be impressed by all our accomplishments if along the way we sacrificed time with them or it cost us our own health? Out of rest and relationships will grow your most lasting and meaningful contributions.

With this foundation in place, I want to share four elements that are helpful for turning vision into reality: your founding myth, your *why*, core values, and defined commitments.

Our Founding Myth

My dad is something of a local legend in Norwood, a mid-sized town near Cincinnati. Our family jokes about it all the time. My parents can't go out to eat or run an errand in their neighborhood without someone coming up to my dad and saying something like, "Hey by any chance are you Gary Rains? You fixed my daughter's car ten years ago." And of course, my super extroverted dad is happy to engage them for a few minutes. If they're lucky, he might also tell them one of his famous marriage jokes. My mom rolls her eyes every time, and there have been lots of times!

But that is what happens when you spend fifty years in one neighborhood fixing cars, usually for multiple generations of drivers in any given family.

The beginnings were much humbler. Dad worked eighty-hour weeks in a slaughterhouse. His days started at 4:00 a.m. in a freezer where he would cut recently killed cattle into pieces of meat. Some days he would have to kill the cattle and hang the carcasses upside down to let the blood drain out, then cut it into pieces that could be sold in stores all while standing in a freezer. It was cold, messy work.

Somewhere along the line it dawned on him that there must be a better way to make money and support his young family! My uncle Gail was a mechanic, working mostly on VW engines, and from time to time he would get asked to do body work. He wasn't interested in collision repair, preferring instead to be under the hood, so he asked my dad if he wanted to give it a try.

Dad was game for about anything at that point. He bought some tools and started reading a book called *Auto Body Repair and Refinishing* by John W. Hogg. That book put me and my sister through college, built a couple churches on the west side of Cincinnati, and made possible hundreds of other great things. In fact, that book coupled with my dad's efforts are literally what built five multimillion-dollar auto body businesses that are still running today.

My dad started fixing VWs on the weekends in a small garage behind our home in South Fairmount, and he got really, really good at it. And he was *fast*. Lightning fast. He developed a system of pre-ordering the parts and painting them before the car showed up. When the weekend came, all he had to do was remove the damaged parts and put the new ones on. He would detail the car with a thorough clean up and return it to the customer all on the same day!

Eventually he had the courage to print business cards that said "Gary's body and paint…same day service on collision repair" and a phone number. The reputation of this little shop grew. Eventually a local Chrysler dealership heard about him and brought him a used car to fix up so they could sell it on their lot. He did his thing. Pre-ordered all the parts, painted them, brought the car in, assembled it, cleaned it. Bam! Same day, back to the dealer.

They didn't even believe it was possible. So they gave him another. Same thing. Again and again. Eventually they hired him to run their whole body shop and service department.

In the late seventies Chrysler ran into some serious problems and went bankrupt. Dad saw the writing on the wall and decided it was time to strike out on his own again. He opened his own body shop a mile down the road, and the rest, as they say, is history.

Your Founding Myth

What I've just shared became our business's founding myth. Every business has a founding myth. If you've been in business for a while, it likely is already there, present in the very DNA of when you started.

Your founding myth helps explain why you started. There was something you wanted to gain, or something you wanted to avoid. Something compelled you to take the risks necessary to launch. And embedded in that story is your founding myth.

Now we have to deal with this word *myth*. Myths are often defined as something that is not really true, something fictional. But in this context, it has more to do with the classic definition. A myth is "a traditional story, especially one concerning the early history of a people or explaining some natural or social phenomenon, and typically involving supernatural beings or events." Myths are simply stories. And it's important to be in touch with yours.

It's also important to note founding myths are often seen more clearly with a little distance. If you are in founding mode, just starting up, it may be hard to land it. You're like a fish in water trying to describe water! It's simply everywhere and everything you know. But as you get some distance and can pan back a bit, your founding myth will become more apparent.

What is your founding myth? What is your origin story? In many ways the founder is the main character. But there's an idea or ideology, a desire, a commitment of some kind that is at the core of your founding story. And it's precisely this that you must tease out over time, this Big Idea that was driving all the early decisions.

Once you understand this, things start to tie together. Things like your values and your vision for the future of the business. Once you deeply know your origin story, it will act as a compass for you and your team as you make decisions daily. It defines who you are, your business's identity.

Your Why

How did you end up in this industry? And possibly a more important question: Why do you stay in it?

Knowing your *why* is like an internal engine that motivates you to achieve more than just getting through the day. It orients you toward a much larger vision and anchors your daily to-do list in something that transcends today. Your *why* differentiates you from your competitors. No two people have the exact same *why*. Some people understand, connect with, and articulate their *why*. But most can't.

I've heard enough stories to know many people feel trapped in their jobs. They wish they'd chosen differently when they were younger. Or they lament not getting the training for what they really love doing. Or maybe their family started before they were ready.

I sympathize, but that's not me.

After spending years working in nonprofits, churches, and even briefly as a social worker investigating cases of child abuse, I feel like my true calling found me. It happened to be the family business my dad had started almost forty years earlier in our backyard as he taught himself how to fix cars from a book. I have always been proud of my dad for starting from scratch in the humble environment of our backyard.

After fifteen years working in nonprofits and churches, how did I end up back in auto body? Well, it came down to money. Not greed, but money. My family was growing and the pay was not keeping pace. Plus, in our community I saw so many projects and dreams fail for lack of just a little funding. It would not have taken much, but time after time I watched little projects falter and then flame out from lack of finances. Good people with a goal to help others. Plenty of vision. Lots of energy and drive. But the funds just were not there to sustain it.

I decided to go back into the family business to make as much money as possible so I could be generous to community organizations in my neighborhood. And that happened to a large extent. I've enjoyed giving to dozens of local nonprofits, organizing "lunch and learns" for the local business community, and helping young entrepreneurs get started on their dreams. What I did not expect was how much I would love this industry and the challenges of growing a local business. Those challenges have served as an enormous benefit as well, as they have kept me interested and intrigued in my trade.

Simon Sinek wrote a book called *Start with Why*. (He also did a great TED talk that summarizes the book really well.) In a nutshell he talks about the importance of having a deep understanding of your *why*.

Usually people start with the *what*. You hear this all the time in the familiar question, "Hey, what do you do?" Our first response might be, "I fix cars."

But there is a deeper level—the *how*. And this is where each of us starts to differentiate ourselves from our competitors. How you fix cars might include things like great customer service or the latest technology, or with great speed and efficiency. These are the kinds of things that set us apart from other shops doing the same type of work.

But there is a deeper level still, and it is truly personal. That is your *why*. Your *why* might be something as simple and noble as feeding, clothing, and sheltering your family. Perhaps your *why* is simply making an honest living or challenging yourself to reach a personal goal. It does not have to be heroic, although it can be. The important thing is that it motivates you and comes from your unique, deeply held desires and beliefs.

Once you start this *why* discovery process, you might find that true motivation, while personal, comes from a *why* that is outside of you, something that calls to you and is much bigger than you. So even though your *why* needs to be deeply personal, consider how what you are doing might improve not only your life but the lives of those around you.

So what is your *why*?

Core Values

For most of my career I didn't understand what it meant to define an organization's values. I have studied leadership for almost thirty years, and I have been in leadership positions for over twenty-five. I've heard people talk about "core values" and how these values guide organizations and form a company's culture. Yet I never quite got it—until a few years ago. I was reading *The Commitment Engine: Making Work Worth It*, by John Jantsch, and I came across this quote:

> The key to creating a great list of commitment beliefs is to throw off any notion of what they should be and simply brainstorm a bit about the best traits of your organization. Think about your people. Who on your team embodies what your company stands for?... This is not a list of what ought to be or what sounds impressive. This is a list of what is, even if what is today isn't as fully developed as you know it can be.

My shop's core values, or what Jantsch calls "commitment beliefs" were already there, present in my shop's culture and history just waiting to be uncovered and highlighted.

Uncovering already existing values seemed so much more doable than trying to write lofty statements that I knew nobody would care about, including me.

Armed with this new insight, I began poking around in our shop and making mental notes of things that were already true about us. I thought back to why I got into the business in the first place. I started asking questions like: What makes us different from other shops? I looked at our advertising and marketing materials.

Soon I came up with a list of several things, including: local generosity, operating with care, serving a higher purpose, environmental stewardship, joy, creativity, and integrity.

This list is more than a bunch of ideals we hope to achieve. These "commitment beliefs" are foundational to who we are—our identity—and they guide everyday decisions like who we hire, how we lead, how and where we spend money, and the stories we tell.

Once you understand your values and have a handful of them, it's important to share them.

Take the Stage

I first heard about the idea of a stump speech from Susan Scott in her book *Fierce Conversations*. Stump speeches started as political messages back in the pioneer days. As early settlers cleared land for farms, stumps were left behind which could be used as mini stages for local politicians to stand on and deliver promises to voters.

Scott encourages executives to stand up regularly in front of their people and as clearly as possible articulate where they're going, why, and how they are going to get there. These three simple points are like an outline for what leaders need to share regularly—at least quarterly—with their teams.

How We Shared Our Values

I remember when we began having monthly team meetings with techs, managers, estimators, and office staff. We intentionally held the meeting in the shop space. Once a month we pulled out the tables and arranged some chairs in our shop. We brought out a simple meal of pizza or BBQ, and we ate and talked.

We started by going around the circle, asking everyone to share one positive thing that happened for them during the past month. It could be related to the shop or something more personal. They shared whatever they wanted. In this way everyone was part of the meeting. Some took it seriously. Others didn't. But everyone was given the opportunity to share anything positive they wanted to share.

Next we shared data. We talked about the financial performance of the shop as a whole, productivity hours for the month, and cycle time. We talked about all the things we measure and track.

Then we usually picked one of our core values and told a story around it. We tried to find something that had happened recently or an important part of our history that illustrated a core value.

One month we talked about local generosity. One of the ways we expressed that was by supporting a local rugby team that was led by my good friend Joshua. Joshua is a firefighter, but in his spare time he loves to teach young people his favorite sport: rugby. And he is passionate about it. Joshua has recruited other coaches and lots of kids through his enthusiasm, and we had the privilege of being a primary financial engine that helped to launch and now sustain it.

During one shop meeting I shared my stump speech on our value of generosity and how it had always been a part of our shop's culture to give. It's in our history. It's in our DNA. I then tied their individual efforts and productivity to our collective ability to be generous toward this local rugby startup. I tried to show them the direct link between what they do on a daily basis and the fact that young men from the neighborhoods we serve are getting mentored and growing their confidence by learning the game of rugby.

So what are your core values, and how do you share them with your team?

Commitments

Now I want to turn to two forms of commitment that will help you push through and beyond the startup stage.

"I Will" Commitments

When I decided to write this book, I knew I needed to do certain things to make sure I got it to the finish line. I wasn't exactly sure what all those actions needed to be or in what order. So I brainstormed a list of possible things that could help me close the gap between this book as an idea and something you are now reading.

I eventually narrowed the list down to a handful of doable actions. I have a friend who used to say, "Do what's doable. It's all you're going to do anyway." I've held on to that idea as I sometimes can get ahead of myself and get really lofty ideas that spiral into the unrealistic and then into the absurd. But here's a few that made the final cut.

- Write 250 words a day. At first this was 1,000. Then it got chopped to 500. Eventually I landed on 250. This was a sustainable word count for me. And certain days I found I could easily exceed it. This was a good

sign that 250 was the right amount to create a sustainable writing habit.
- Hire a collaborator/editor. I hired Chad Allen (www.chadrallen.com), who helped develop the manuscript and prepare it for publication.
- Review and repeat my identity mantra on a daily basis: "I am a respected author, mentor, teacher, and coach."
- Listen to select podcasts on a daily basis that will give me ideas, stories, and direction for my daily writing.

Sticking with these commitments must have worked because you're now reading the book! I used this tactic many times in my business as well.

What challenge or big goal are you facing at the moment? Is there a way you can break that down into smaller steps? What is the simplest next action you could take? What tiny step might create some momentum in the right direction?

"I Won't" Commitments

It is equally important to commit to *not* do certain things that get in the way of our goals. What actions or activities need to be pruned from your life in order to make room for what you want to accomplish?

Using my example again of writing this book, I decided on an "I won't" commitment: "I won't turn on my phone until I've written 250 words."

I wanted to turn my phone on, so this now became a reward for completing an assignment that would eventually lead to this book. I knew if I could just wake up and write 250 words every day, eventually a book would naturally emerge. Of course, there are many other steps to writing a book—editing, publishing, marketing, etc. But if you don't have words, you don't have a book.

What do you need to start doing ("I will") and stop doing ("I won't") to help you reach your goals?

With a strong understanding of your founding myth, clarity on why you do what you do, and deeply internalizing your core values and commitments, you have the necessary foundation to build out your dream.

4

CHAOS

How to Grow Your Business and Work through Your Growing Pains

RUNNING A BUSINESS is hard. And confusing. At least it was for me.

In 2002 I rejoined the family business of auto body repair. After about a year of working for my father, we decided it was time for me to launch out on my own. With a severe case of naive optimism, I launched a small shop near my home. It wasn't long before the reality check hit me. Hard.

I remember sitting in my office, staring at a wall, terrified. What have I done? To launch this business, an auto body shop, I borrowed money from my parents for the down payment and the rest from a bank. All I had at the start was several hundred thousand dollars of debt, an empty building, and a lot of fear. Throw in a little confusion and a bewildered "How did I get here?" look and you have a pretty good idea of how things were going at that point.

There were only a couple cars in the shop. I had no idea how I was going to pay my vendors, pay the bank, pay my dad, pay my team, or pay myself. The few cars we had in the shop were not enough for the upcoming week of bills, let alone the ones that would be due in a couple weeks as we rolled into another month! I distinctly remember that moment staring blankly at the wall, paralyzed with fear and having no idea what to do next.

At the time I was bi-vocational. I was running a business to support my family so I could be about my "real" calling, which was ministry. I was *very* prepared for ministry and very unprepared to lead a business. I studied Bible and theology in college and graduate school. I even got a doctorate of ministry. Fancy, right? Well, none of that taught me anything about marketing, growing sales, or how I was going to make payroll or pay my bills this week!

Just in the Nick of Time... A Breakthrough

Out of sheer desperation I did what nearly everyone else does when they reach this point: I prayed and I Googled. The prayer was not eloquent, but it was heartfelt. It was more of a "Lord, if you get me out of this..." prayer than anything else. You know, the kind where you bargain and promise to live better, make better choices.

Then I Googled. I Googled "small business marketing." I figured if I could just get enough jobs in the door, I could figure things out from there. At the time a curious name kept coming up: Duct Tape Marketing. I dug a little deeper to discover that the man behind that curious name was John Jantsch.

I started reading and studying everything I could find from John. I followed him on social media. I read his blog, scouring it for free ideas. He had a course called "Referral Flood" that was $19. I figured I could afford that and maybe I would learn something that would lead me to some new work. I devoured it! I read it like my life depended on it. I applied everything I could from it. One of his ideas was to join a BNI chapter. BNI stands for Business Network International. Each chapter hosts a structured weekly meeting where various business leaders come together to share about what they offer and to give and get referrals.

I looked up BNI and was stoked to learn there was a meeting just a mile away from my shop! I reached out to the leader of the group, Stacy. She invited me to come and see for myself if it would be a good fit. I put on a sport coat and headed out the next morning to their 7:00 a.m. meeting. The room was packed and full of energy. Once things got started, we went around the room and each person gave a 60-second commercial explaining what they did and what kind of referrals they were looking for. I shared a bit about my business, and I think I made a joke about what kind of referrals I wanted saying something like, "I'm looking for introductions to bad drivers."

The last part of the meeting everyone went around again. This time each talked about what referrals they could give or introductions to prospective clients they could make for others. One woman in the group who sold office furniture said, "I can give Kevin a referral." I wasn't expecting that! "I wrecked my car a month ago and the shop where it's at hasn't touched it in a month! Kevin, if you give me your address, I'll have them tow it to your shop." Whoa! My first meeting, and I get an actual job out of it! I had no idea what kind of job it was, but it felt like I was on to something. Turns out it was a $14,000 insurance claim—almost seven times the size of my average repair order at that time. It also represented about half of the revenue I needed for the month. Yeah, BNI was definitely for me!

There were some other early wins as well that taught me important lessons. Like the time a student from a nearby university ran across the hoods of eight Volkswagens at the dealer across the street. We couldn't even handle all eight at once, so they gave four to us and four to another shop nearby. We made a point to repair, paint, and detail all four of ours as quickly as possible and get them back to them. We wanted to show them that even though we were a tiny shop, we were capable of handling jobs quickly and efficiently. The big learning there was figuring out who gets to your customers before you do and partnering with them. That led to a relationship with that dealer that eventually turned into about $300,000 of recurring, annual income. For context, that was more revenue than the entire shop made annually during our first couple of years.

As I continued to grow my referral network, I also started working on getting insurance contracts. For the first five years or so I didn't have any. But then a shop near me messed up and got kicked off an insurance program, so they gave us a shot. That ended up being a contract worth almost a million dollars of annual revenue at my first location. And I was able to keep that same contract at all the shops I acquired, five in total. In the end, that one insurance contract gave us several million dollars of recurring, yearly revenue. Just as importantly, it led to us getting other contracts. It seemed like our marketing was on autopilot.

All in all, that little neighborhood shop multiplied ten times in ten years. When I acquired it, it did about $250,000 in annual revenue, supporting about three team members, a couple technicians, and me. I was doing everything except fixing the cars. I wrote the estimates, ordered the parts, paid the bills, and dealt with the insurance adjusters. In the afternoons I was often the head detailer as well! But I'm grateful for those humble beginnings. I learned the business from the ground up, touching every aspect of it. I had no interest in mastering them all, but learning them was important. After ten years I looked up and realized we were doing close to $2.5 million in annual revenue and had moved into a much bigger facility. We started by fixing about ten cars a month. After ten years we were fixing over a hundred monthly.

At this point, I started to wonder if we could multiply ten times again. I had no idea how, but I figured "Why not?" We had grown ten times once. I was sure we could figure it out. At that point I started to acquire other shops. By the time I sold in 2021—exactly eighteen years after we started—we had five locations and our run rate was over $1 million per month in combined revenue. We had grown fifty times in those eighteen years.

To say it was a smooth process would be worse than a stretch—it would be an all-out lie. We encountered *a lot* of chaos as we grew. But as difficult as chaos can be, it's actually a good thing—one of the natural pains of a growing business. We'll talk about how to address chaos later in this chapter, but what if your business is not growing? What then? Let me suggest some possible culprits as well as solutions for each.

The Power of Simplicity

One source of stagnation or lack of growth is complexity. I was coaching a leader this week on achieving his goals. He was getting "lost in the sauce," as cooks say. He was making things much harder than they needed to be. What he needed was some sales momentum. We started talking about all the things he might do to get that. We talked about social media ads. We explored online reviews. We discussed referral strategies.

Somehow, we started to drift into finances. We began discussing a weekly financial snapshot. We talked about simplifying his financial reporting and how it could be more visual. Then it hit me! Wait, we've drifted here. We intended to talk about sales momentum. Now we're into finances. Also, the sales ideas we came up with were time-consuming and somewhat complicated.

So I asked him, "What is the one thing you can do today that would help you to land more jobs? Think about something that wouldn't cost you anything and you could do in ten minutes a day, every day." That was a tall order in my mind to check all those boxes! But he immediately said, "I could call the last three people I wrote estimates for." Boom! That was it. That cut out all the clutter, all the wasted steps, all the complications. Just pick up the phone and call potential customers who have already asked for an estimate. I followed up with him the next day. He landed one of the three and was committed to doing it again. And again. If he gets one more job a day, it will revolutionize his profits.

A lot of shop owners are familiar with the concept of "Lean." One of the most foundational concepts in "Lean" is eliminating waste. Most processes we engage in on a daily basis are littered with unnecessary, oftentimes complicated steps. Those extra steps are a prime example of waste. If your goal is x, do you really need to do a, b, c, d, all the way to x? Or can you somehow go from a to x in one grand step? Sometimes the answer is no. Sometimes there need to be three or four or more steps to do something right. However, my goal with my coaching clients is to make things as simple and easy as possible while getting the results they want.

What if you could bypass most of the steps in your current project or goal? What if that process you're working on only needed three steps instead of eight? What if you could get the same result in one-tenth the time and effort?

To some, this might sound lazy. It might sound like I want to skip to the good parts as quickly and easily as possible! (I do!) Others might say I'm advocating for impatience. Like I don't want to waste a lot of time! (I don't!) Here's the thing: Processes and projects have what my contractor calls "scope creep." The scope—meaning the complexity, time, and money required—tends to grow over time. It actually takes a lot of effort and discipline to keep things as simple as possible.

My friend Greg used to tell me I was the "Chief Intuitive Leaper" of my shops. It was a made-up title, of course. But he was trying to communicate that I could often find a way to leap to the last step and get the same or 80 percent of the result without following all the steps in between, saving loads of time, effort, and even money. It took me a while to unpack all that it meant, but now I see that title as a badge of honor. I'm proud I can often help businesses get the results they need faster, with less waste and less expense.

So what are you working on that could be trimmed, simplified, and cleaned up? There is great power in simplicity. It just might lead you to more growth than you ever imagined.

Learning to Let Go

Another possible limit on growth is when the owner-leader is holding on to too much responsibility. I remember a time early on when I went away for a short vacation. We were only a few years in at that point. I remember going away and feeling far from the business. It was great to relax with my family. It was also a real ego boost when I returned and the first thing my assistant said to me was, "We're so glad you're back! This place just doesn't run the same without you!" I swelled with pride. It felt so good to be needed!

But then a sense of terror started to creep in as I realized, "Oh no! This place doesn't run the same without me!" It dawned on me: I had not built a business. I had only given myself a job. Only when our businesses can run without us do we actually have a business. Deep down we want our businesses to run the same whether we are there or not. Once that is true, we are free from our business and things can start to go on autopilot.

Early on it is normal that our businesses will only operate well when we are there. However, if we want to go from "I've got a job" to "I've got a business," we have to make sure the business can run without us being the center of everything. And let me be clear up front that just because we do not remain the center of our business, this does not mean we don't have an important role to play. But it's the difference between being the parent of a newborn, the parent of a teenager, the parent of an adult child, and a grandparent. I've been all of those. And it's like the old adage says, "If I knew how good being a grandparent was going to be I would have never been a parent and just skipped ahead to being a grandparent." We all know it doesn't work like that!

Dependency is a necessary stop along the way, but I encourage you to not get stuck there. Your ego and pride may want you to always be the center of attention, but that is the only reward. And it's an exhausting reward if you don't move beyond it. We must become detached from our business for its own good and ultimately ours as well.

How do we do this? First, we need clear job descriptions for all the key functions our business needs to thrive, including the name of who fills each role. Now, your name may be in all or most at first. But eventually the goal is to hire, train, or outsource all the roles that fall outside what Dan Sullivan calls your "unique ability."

For example, I *hated* doing the bookkeeping and finance part of my business. I didn't understand it very well and could just do the basics of paying my bills by using a folder system. When a bill came in, it went into the left side of a two-pocket folder. When it was paid, I marked it paid and moved it to the right side of the folder. Then when the month was over and the bills were paid, I archived the old folder and got a new one.

Because I hate paying bills and doing this rudimentary bookkeeping, that was the first job description and process I developed and handed off as soon as I could afford it. I hired my wife! It quickly became apparent this was not her "unique ability" either, so eventually I outsourced it to an actual bookkeeper. As my business grew, I eventually hired a controller, then a CFO to handle all this in a much more thorough and sophisticated way, but it started by me being honest about what I loved doing, admitting it wasn't finance, packaging that into a process and job description, and hiring others as soon as I was able.

Pushing through the Resistance

When my youngest daughter was learning to drive, she kept saying, "I don't feel like I'll ever get to drive on my own!" It felt like an endless number of practice hours, driving school, and just waiting until she turned seventeen. One day I got sick of her telling me how she felt because I knew her desired autonomy was coming soon, and it would feel like it was worth the wait and the effort. "Tell your feelings to go to hell!" I told her. I was stunned even as the words came out of my mouth, but looking back, I don't think it was bad advice.

Dallas Willard said feelings are great servants but horrible masters, and he was right. Listen, when you feel like you'll never get there and the business might fail, consider telling your feelings to go to hell and keep doing the work. Write the next paragraph. Fix the next car. Refinish the next floor. Build the next wall. Style the next head of hair. Just keep doing the next right thing, and that day of prosperity will dawn!

In the auto body industry, we have a saying: things have to get worse before they get better. In other words, before something can be fixed, it has to enter an even more chaotic state. Like before we could properly fix a panel, we had to disassemble the areas around it making it "worse" so that we could access the areas we needed to make better.

This is true for a lot of creative endeavors! Think about painting a room, for example. All that sanding and taping and priming makes things look just awful before that final coat brings it all together. Or imagine telling your barber to stop cutting your hair halfway through. Yikes!

Just like in the messy process of painting a room or getting a haircut, taking on substantial endeavors often means facing some daunting challenges. At some point we hit a wall. All of us. Me. You. Everyone who attempts anything worth attempting, whether it be writing, painting, or launching a business will meet the wall.

At first it looks impassable and impossible. We begin to think there is no way over, under, or around this behemoth! So we stand and stare. We start to talk ourselves out of whatever we intended to accomplish. All the reasons we won't succeed start to surface. What our third-grade teacher said about our inability to follow through. What our junior-high coach said about not having what it takes to actually win. What our parents told us in subtle ways by encouraging us to settle. We think of every person real and imagined who told us we weren't enough. Not smart enough. Not strategic enough. Not good enough. Just not enough.

This is the perfect time to quit, we think, to admit defeat. We're tempted to believe that by doing so we are coming to our senses.

The roadblocks are legion. In the body shop industry, it might be the insurance companies trying to gain control of the repair process. Or the complexity of the new cars—how they are like driving computers and can't be fixed like in the old days. Or maybe it's the complexity of online marketing and not understanding Google's algorithm. Maybe it's the customers you worked tirelessly to please and they still give you a one-star review. There are and will always be thousands of reasons to turn around. To give up and give in. To go get a job and stop trying to act like you can be a business owner.

If you're feeling resistance, that's actually good news—you're probably on the right path. Resistance often signifies that you're pursuing something meaningful. If all you feel is joy and everything is always rainbows and unicorns, you might be on a track that leads nowhere. Think of resistance as a guide, teaching you that you're aligned with a worthy goal. It's a critical part of the journey to success.

Remember, resistance can't be simply bypassed; it must be overcome daily. If you're encountering it, chances are you've found an endeavor worth giving your all. The path won't be smooth; it'll resemble a rocky mountain range with highs and lows. But the aim is that your overall direction will be upward.

The Power of Unless

As a business owner, I can attest there is an ebb and flow to revenue. Often the factors that drive business can seem completely out of our control. So with that as backdrop, picture this: It's the last day of the month, and I'm talking with one of our production managers.

"Hey, Tom, it looks like we're not going to hit our monthly number," I said.

Awkward silence.

"Tom, are you still there?" I waved my hand in front of his face.

"Yeah, I'm just thinking how I want to respond," he said. "I guess I just feel like it's all my fault. Like maybe I'm just not doing a good enough job."

This is where many leaders go: the Shame Game.

"Well, I know you're putting the effort in! And the last thing I want you to do is go to a dark place right now! That won't help anyone, especially you," I offered. "I'm curious, what else might it be?"

"Well," Tom responded, "Jim said he heard from some parts delivery guy that it's slow everywhere. Maybe there just wasn't enough work out there to go around this month. Or maybe it's the big consolidators that just came to town. I heard they got all these big contracts with the insurance companies that have been steering all the work to them. I don't know, really."

Now Tom had a full head of steam. If it wasn't his fault, it had to be something completely out of his control, right?

Listen, the Shame Game's no good, but the Blame Game doesn't help much either! The Blame Game defeats learning and taking action. Blaming things outside of our direct control creates a self-defeating cycle. The very tools we most need when things get tough—creativity and taking action—get stripped away by the Blame and Shame Games.

But I've found a way out. It's changing the game with one word, a word I referred to in the introduction: "unless." When we hear ourselves or others going to blame or shame, we simply add the word "unless" to the end of the sentence and try to think of other possible solutions. Let's see what happens when we apply "unless" to the ideas Tom expressed.

- "I guess I'll just never be good enough to be a production manager! Maybe I should just find another job that better suits me... unless... I took some training classes in production management or found a mentor from another location who has gone from newbie to mastery of this role."
- "We can't compete with the MSO consolidators and their massive marketing budgets and insurance contracts... unless... we use our local and family-owned status as a marketing advantage."

Sometimes when we feel defeated, like there's nothing we can do to overcome our current situation, all we need is one simple, magic word to unlock the possibilities: "unless."

What current challenge are you facing? How might "unless" help you discover a new opportunity lurking in the shadows of blame or shame?

From Chaos to Order

In the opening verses of Scripture, we can learn a lot about how God works: "In the beginning God created the heavens and the earth. The earth was formless and empty, and darkness covered the deep waters. And the Spirit of God was hovering over the surface of the waters" (Genesis 1:1–2 NLT). We learn that the Spirit of God hovered over chaos, over disorder. A major part of the creation story is God bringing order out of chaos. Do you think of your work this way?

Essentially all work is bringing order out of chaos. In my work repairing wrecked cars, I saw the disorder and chaos of an auto accident. There's bent metal, broken plastic, and often fluids spilling from the car when it is towed to a shop. Our job was to remove the broken parts, install new parts, and paint and detail the car to restore it to its intended order and beauty.

What is the chaos you are ordering? If you are a school teacher, you are ordering young minds. If you are a house cleaner, you are ordering rooms where people live. If you are a family counselor, you are bringing order to broken relationships. If you are a dentist, you are bringing order to decaying or broken teeth. Whatever role you have, I'm sure there is an element of ordering chaos.

Another form of chaos is what happens when our business is growing beyond our ability to keep up. This form can be especially maddening because of how desperately we want to serve our customers well.

The good news is we have a God who is an expert at ordering chaos. He wants to help and guide you as you bring order today. He is right there ready to guide and help you with any project that needs to be organized or relationship that needs to be restored.

What chaos are you ordering today and how might you invite God as your expert advisor to help you?

Having covered some sources of chaos, we'll now turn to some ways you can bring order to the chaos, starting with finding your copilot.

Find Your Copilot

Henry David Thoreau once wrote, "If you have built castles in the air, your work need not be lost; that is where they should be. Now, put the foundations under them."

As a self-professed visionary, I relate to the first half of that quote so well. I have blueprints to many a castle tucked away in my mind. I carried dreams for my shops for many years. I could see what the future of our shops looked like. I could even sense what it was going to feel like when we arrived at that ever-elusive, but highly desirable future. I knew our *why*. I knew I wanted to give away $1 million to abused, abandoned, and orphaned children. I knew I wanted to have well-equipped shops, staffed by energetic people who love coming to work in this industry. I knew how many team members I ultimately wanted and how many shops. I had a strong idea of where our shops would be located. The *what*, the *why*, and the *who* were very clear to me.

It's the *how*—the foundation in real life—that tripped me up. I was certain of the future; it was the present that often left me perplexed—until I found a copilot.

Turns out, I wasn't supposed to have the answer! I'm not even wired for it. What a freeing thought that was! I didn't have to have all the answers. Why? Because that was someone else's job, someone else's gift, someone else's wiring. And I found him several years after starting my business. His name is Keith Foster, and he became my chief operating officer. Although that's his title, his role was better described by what the authors of the book *Rocket Fuel* call an "integrator."

Rocket Fuel teaches there are two types of leaders needed for any entrepreneurial enterprise that wants to scale rapidly: visionaries and integrators. Their job descriptions are very different.

Visionaries tend to live in the future, have big ideas (most of which should never see the light of day!), handle key partner relationships, design and build out the culture and values, pursue fresh opportunities (like acquisitions), and are the face of the brand.

Integrators, on the other hand, keep all the trains running on time. They love to create processes and build systems that empower teams to achieve results. They are great at installing structure, discipline, repetition, and accountability.

To be clear, Keith was not easy to find. When I described to a couple of well-known industry consultants what I was looking for, one of them said, "Oh, I get it now! You're looking for a unicorn." My original criteria did seem very unrealistic. I wanted someone with decades of industry experience, who lived within an hour of me, and who had already scaled an operation from a handful of shops to over ten locations. But Keith checked all the boxes, and I hired him.

What did this mean for me? In a word: freedom. I was free again to be full time in the visionary seat—to imagine the future and put the rough draft in place. I had my dream job again! All the stuff that was so confounding to me, Keith seemed to do with ease. All of a sudden I was excited about the industry and my enterprise in ways I had never experienced. I literally couldn't wait to get up and get going every day to see what new muscle my enterprise would develop under Keith's leadership and what new opportunity or relationship was coming down the pike for me to discover and nurture. Let me assure you, with the right pairing of visionary and integrator, just about anything is possible for your business.

Board of Advisors

We are raised in a culture of the rugged individualists—the person who goes it alone, makes their own path, never showing any signs of weakness.

Well, even though I'll admit it's hard for me to ask for help, I think that's bunk. The myth of the self-made man or woman is just that: myth. We are all born dependent little creatures, and even as we gain independence, we never outgrow our need for help of some kind. The sooner we can embrace this—and I'm preaching to myself here—the sooner we can get the help we need.

So when I need help, where do I turn?

I love to read, so I typically find a book. This is how I initially learned about search engine optimization. I have also engaged the services of many coaches and consultants. Some of them have been for free, as I just asked friends who knew something I didn't. And of course, there are the seminars, webinars, workshops, and conferences both inside and outside the industry that I have attended.

But at the end of 2010, I stumbled upon an idea that might trump all of the above—an advisory board. Here is how my board came together.

First, I started looking around in the circles I was already in to see if there were people who shared my values and had done what I wanted to do. For me, that boiled down to people who had significantly grown a small business and lived lives that demonstrated values of family, faith, generosity, and community service. It was a tall order, but once I laid out that criteria and started looking, it took me less than a month to find five people who fit the bill.

One I met through my church, another through a weekly networking group, another owned a business less than a mile away, another was someone with whom I had lots of mutual friends and whom I got to know over a few lunches before extending the invitation.

In all, I identified five people I wanted to ask just to see what they would say. My expectations were to meet quarterly as a group for a couple of hours to discuss the financial strength of my business, hold me accountable to goals I had set, and advise me on specific challenges my shop was facing. The initial commitment would be for one year. To my surprise, they all said yes.

You might wonder if I paid these folks. At first I did not pay these kind, generous souls, but as the business grew we sent them a bonus at Christmas time.

We had a standardized quarterly agenda that revolved around three things: my shop's financials, progress toward stated goals, and questions I was currently asking. That last one was the most free-form and usually involved something I felt stuck on or perhaps a situation I was too close to and needed perspective on.

As the meeting approached, I usually asked my managers if they thought there was anything to put on the agenda. They almost always had great suggestions.

The board helped me in at least two ways. The first was with specific input on needed changes. For example, when I wanted to introduce a bonus plan in the shop, I proposed to the board that we give bonuses to the team based on overall sales. The board encouraged me to rethink that. They suggested I not base everyone's bonus on the same thing, as many of the team did not have direct control over sales, so they would not be able to tie their efforts to the bonus.

The board challenged me to have a more sophisticated bonus structure that was simultaneously tied to cycle time, quality of repairs, and overall throughput. They encouraged me to consider not making the bonus all or nothing, but instead more of a graded bonus that could be partially awarded for targets met. I ended up with a dynamic bonus plan that was much better than I initially envisioned.

Another key benefit I experienced from my board was confidence. They affirmed several decisions I wanted to make. Prior to having a board, I often felt like I was making decisions in a vacuum. With the board I could consult with them and walk away confident that the decision was backed by several people who have loads of experience and my best interests in mind. This allowed me to make hard decisions with great confidence.

Both/And Management

For many years I had an ongoing, internal debate raging: Is it possible to be a kind and caring leader and still be effective? The models of leadership I inherited from a family with generational roots in the military hold that leaders can choose to be either kind and ineffective or demanding and effective. But is there a third way? A both/and?

I want to admit upfront that in an effort to challenge the notion that only highly demanding leaders can be effective, I often overswing. I have overcompensated with a kinder, gentler approach.

I think I have proven to myself that different approaches to leadership can work as I've crafted a style of leadership that tends toward the kind and gentle all while growing my business fifty times over eighteen years.

What I also learned, though, is that any approach can be taken too far and become a weakness. There truly is a shadow side to the kinder, gentler approach, if it's not kept in check. I've also become aware that my internal "kindness vs. demanding" debate is a false dichotomy. It's not an either/or—it's a both/and. Several books in recent years like *Fierce Conversations, Radical Candor,* and *Crucial Conversations* discuss the creative tension of this "both/and" approach. The authors affirm that being kind and understanding while holding your team to a high standard is more effective than one or the other. Both are needed.

Flattery is another part of the shadow side of encouragement. Flattery is not really about helping the other person do a great job or develop their skills. Rather, flattery is for us. It actually is a tool of manipulation. We flatter people so they will like us and do what we want them to do. Flattery is what unchecked encouragement and kindness can turn into.

Kindness must be kept in check with things like holding your team accountable and having hard conversations when effort and performance lag. Calling those you lead to become great and holding them to a higher standard is actually the most caring thing you, as a leader, can do. They will become better for it.

Consider these questions:

Do you tend to be more empathetic or harsh during conversations? How can you better balance this?

What is a hard conversation you have been avoiding? What is holding you back from having it? Is it fear, and if so, fear of what? How might you at least start that conversation today?

Free Leadership Guide

I created a guide to help you become both an authoritative and gentle leader. Download it for free at **www.rainslegacy.co**

Getting Personal with Your Team

This is going to be a section that many will not agree with. So be it.

I have become convinced that to build a strong culture, leaders have to get personally close to their team. There, I said it. This flies in the face of so much advice we hear from attorneys and human resource professionals. They warn us to keep a safe distance from our team members and not to ask too many questions. We are told, for instance, that if we ask about an employee's health and then have to fire them for some other valid reason shortly after, they might bring a labor lawsuit against us claiming it was because they divulged some health concerns. Okay, fair enough. That is a valid, albeit worst-case, scenario.

But think about it another way. What are the costs of not getting close to your team? What are the costs of them feeling like no one really cares about them as a person? What are the risks of treating our team members like numbers? I would argue those costs are much higher. There's an old saying that people don't leave jobs; they leave bosses. If you don't care for them, perhaps someone else is just waiting for the opportunity.

Santiago Jaramillo and Todd Richardson, in their book *Agile Engagement*, contend that "long-term management success depends on caring for the whole employee, including his or her personal life. You only unlock your full leadership potential, thoroughly engage employees, and achieve maximum business success if you get personal with your employees and care about both their professional and personal interests."

I distinctly remember benefiting greatly from the gift of new team members because certain shops in my area were not taking care of their people. And in all fairness, I'm sure other shops benefited when I did not care for my team members as I should have.

Now it may be because of how I'm wired. Some may even consider this a flaw or bad strategy. But I decided to care for my team as people and get as personal as they would allow.

For those of you who are willing to take that risk, read on. I want to try to answer this question: How do we care for our team both personally and professionally in such a way that they will be happy and productive at work?

There are two major ways to make your culture more personal and more personally meaningful.

MBWA: Managing by Walking Around

There's an old proverb: If one person says you have a tail, they are crazy. If two people say you have a tail, it's a conspiracy and people have decided to mess with you. If seven people say you have a tail, you'd better turn around and check!

You may very well have a tail—not a literal one but one that takes other people out.

A practical way to hear from others about your blind spots is to use a method called "managing by walking around." MBWA for short.

This leadership style was popularized many years ago, but it's still relevant today. And quite simple. All you do is, well, walk around. Get out on the front lines of your business. Talk directly with some team members. Spend a couple hours working alongside a technician. Ask questions. And then listen. Really listen.

Here are a few things to keep in mind as you start this practice.

I often took a lap around my shops and tried to talk one-on-one to as many team members as possible. Typically, this was about 80 percent personal and 20 percent business. I asked them about their family and their hobbies mostly. These two topics alone generate plenty of fodder for these brief but hopefully meaningful encounters.

You can also ask for feedback, but be careful. It's easy for this to turn into putting out fires or pointing out flaws or meddling with "fixes" that don't really help. The point is to be present, not with all the answers, but simply with an open mind, ready to learn from those doing the core work of the business.

This posture of listening and learning requires a strong mix of humility, confidence, and curiosity. Ask your team what they think could be done better or differently.

Try out a few questions like:

"What could we do to make your job easier?"

"What can I do to be a better leader?"

It's one thing to walk around to try to "manage" people. It's another to walk around to learn about your team, to gain insight into how you're leading, and to discover what the needs of the front line are. The first just requires getting out into the weeds of the business, the front lines. The latter requires the humility of a learning posture and a servant's heart.

Memorable Moments

Another key way to care for your team is by creating meaningful and memorable moments. Authors Chip and Dan Heath in their new book, *The Power of Moments: Why Certain Experiences Have Extraordinary Impact*, contend that our minds do not remember all moments equally, but instead retain certain experiences that stand out above the others. How do we create these moments? They identified four key elements that create defining, memorable moments:

- elevation
- insight
- pride
- connection

Let's dive deeper.

Elevation: "Defining moments rise above the everyday," the authors write. Defining moments are filled with a sense of surprise and they lead to joy.

Insight. Defining moments consist of an "a-ha" where we experience a new insight or understand something old in a new way.

Pride. According to the Heath brothers, "defining moments capture us at our best—moments of achievement, moments of courage."

Connection. Defining moments are often social and relational. Defining moments are meaningful for having been shared with others.

One way our team nurtured defining and memorable moments was with "atta boys" and "atta girls" accolades during our shop meetings. We took time at many of our meetings to "catch people doing something right" and praise them for it publicly. This did not come just from the managers to the employees. It was an open forum where anyone could say something positive about anyone else. I'm sure you can see how this simple practice connects to all four of the key elements above.

Yes, there are risks to getting too personal with your team. But there are great rewards as well. If you are willing to take the risk and put in the work, I'm confident you will reap many rewards from a more engaged team.

Hiring and Developing

One of the most rewarding aspects of being a business owner is watching people develop and progress in their careers. I've had the chance to see a number of my team members grow within the industry, and it's one of the things I was most proud of in my shop.

However, when hiring, it can feel difficult—even impossible—to accurately identify and choose those goal-oriented, driven people who can take an opportunity and turn it into a career.

An example: One of my techs, Mike, came to me with just a little experience from a production shop. Over many years he acquired the tools, knowledge, and skill to move from being an apprentice fixing small dents to a true A-level technician who can handle any job I throw at him.

Then there's Jason. My father hired him right out of vocational school at our family's original shop, and he literally started out at the ground level sweeping floors and prepping cars. Eventually he came with me to help launch my shop and went from prepping and painting on his own to estimating and, eventually, to managing a large crew. When he started with me, we were only doing about ten cars a month. Ten years later he was managing our whole team, pulling closer to a hundred vehicles a month.

Mike and Jason are both examples of guys hired from within the industry—young repair professionals looking for an opportunity to grow.

But is there ever a time when it's a good idea to hire from outside the industry?

Chris, who served as our general manager, had been my friend for many years. Before coming into our business, Chris earned a doctorate degree in leadership and worked as both a school administrator and a professor at a local college. He is an expert at leading and teaching; his experience and education back that up.

Yet Chris had no industry experience at all and had to learn the business from the ground up—but not in the same way that someone coming from vocational school would. Yes, I wanted him to get his hands dirty from time to time, turning a wrench or trying his hand at painting. He also needed to be able to write a decent estimate. However, I did not hire him for his technical skill. I hired him for his ability to help us create the culture and team that my business needed at that point in our development.

Early on in my career, I thought I had to hire "Swiss Army Knife" employees—guys who could do anything from frames to paint to writing proper estimates. We sometimes jokingly, but also with real admiration, called these guys "Walking

Body Shops." They were versatile and wanted to learn everything from top to bottom.

But as our shop grew from just a couple employees to a team of almost twenty people, the culture shifted to specialists—men and women who go after a deep mastery of a particular role.

We kept a couple Swiss Army Knives around, and we tried to cross train whenever possible, but as we grew I discovered the kind of person who is really good at QuickBooks is not necessarily the best person to prep and paint cars. And it rarely makes sense to push them to do both.

I often heard how hard it is for shops to find talent—and I agreed! It was not easy. However, the talent you are looking for might be right in front of you and is just waiting for an opportunity, or perhaps they are in a completely different field but looking to make a change.

Sometimes talent is hiding in plain sight. If we are willing to take the time and risk to develop it or ask for it, we might realize it was there all along.

5

CONTROLS

Practices to Build Momentum in Your Business

For the visionary entrepreneur, a chapter on controls can feel like a real downer. "I want freedom to create things, change things up! The idea of controls is so BORING!"

It's a bit of a paradox, but controls are actually the things that create freedom and allow for even more creativity to flourish. In this chapter I'll show you how.

And it all starts with checklists.

The Mighty Power of the Modest Checklist

Checklists are often not taken seriously because they are so simple. Sure, they're great for grocery shopping, but are they really useful for running a business? Shouldn't everyone just know their job and do it correctly time after time?

In his book *The Checklist Manifesto*, Atul Gawande, a surgeon who routinely performs life-or-death procedures, emphasizes the importance of checklists among doctors and nurses. He points out pilots use checklists before each and every takeoff. Why? Because checklists save lives.

Now the stakes in your business are likely not as life-or-death as flying an airplane or performing surgeries. Nevertheless, in the auto body industry and many others, the quality control portion of completing a job can be reduced to a checklist. A closely followed checklist can save a lot of frustration.

Handoffs from one department to another also benefit from checklists. For us, a car moved from the person who wrote the estimate to the technician. A checklist proved very helpful to make sure that everything got communicated. Likewise, when a car moved from the body shop to the paint department—another handoff—a checklist brought clarity and confirmed that the car was ready for paint. Ditto from paint to clean up. And again, from clean up to delivery. Having in-process checklists for each handoff brought clarity and eased each transition.

Developing Your Playbook

I hate fixing the same problem over and over, so when I was in the auto body business, I got decent at coming up with simple solutions to seemingly complex problems. And usually, once I fixed a problem, I could get others on board and it would stick.

What I didn't do so well was document the solution. When I did document it, I wouldn't remember where I documented it. Was it in Google Drive? Email? Was there a hard copy floating around the bottom of my junk drawer? This became a problem when we started to scale. If I was there, it wasn't a problem. I could remember and reinforce it. But as soon as I had to be in two places at once, there was no second me to reinforce it, so we were fixing the same problems again and again. One of the fathers of total quality management, W. Edwards Deming, said, "Blame the process, not the people."

In 2016 a movie called *The Founder* came out about the early days of the McDonald's franchise. It was fascinating. If ever there was a company that has perfected processes as much as humanly possible, it's McDonald's. They consistently churn out the same exact product in hundreds of diverse countries across thousands of locations for millions of people every day. The idea that you can get the exact same hamburger with no variation in Denver as you can get in Hong Kong on any given day is astounding. Amazingly, that burger can be made by a teenager recently trained and working for minimum wage! That's process at its finest. McDonald's does not depend on the genius of individuals. It rests solely on the genius of process.

Much like sports teams develop a playbook for various ways the opponent is trying to beat them, we need a playbook for the issues and problems that come up in our business. If I could start my businesses all over again, this would be one of the top three things I would do differently. Why? Because I believe documenting and enforcing processes is the only way to scale without creating more chaos as we grow.

Here's the process I recommend:

1. Solve an issue or problem one time.
2. Document that solution in one place.
3. Hire, fire, or train people based on this documented solution.
4. Check up on the person and the process for compliance.
5. If upon inspection they have found a better way, make that the new standard and reward them!

I'll be honest. This process can feel tedious and boring. Who wants to take the time not only to solve a problem but document it too? It's also time-consuming, initially. If solving the problem takes an hour, let's say documenting it takes five hours. That may seem like a lot, but I'm telling you, those five hours will save you thousands of hours in the long run.

Documenting processes will take some time, but let me assure you, you don't need a massive playbook. Focus on documenting the handful of core processes that really drive your business. And think of documenting core processes as itself a core process. It's one of those fundamentals you ignore to your own detriment. Can you run a business without this fundamental? Sure, but it will make your life more difficult and your business less profitable.

Following through on the Fundamentals

I'm not a college football fan. So when I write this name, please don't tune me out if you like a rival team. I'm only interested in this guy because of how he leads and because one of my managers was a big fan of his. Ready? Nick Saban.

Nick Saban was the highly intense and often controversial head coach of the Alabama Crimson Tide football team. What I have come to love and admire about Nick Saban was his focused intensity on getting the fundamentals right. Over and over again he drilled his team not to focus on the score but how to execute the next play that is right here, right now. His maniacal focus on doing the right thing play after play was what separated him from the pack. And make no mistake—he was separated from the pack. It's like he coached and played in his own league. He led his team to four national championships and groomed some great NFL players still playing today.

Saban's disciplined approach appeals to me precisely because it is what I lack. When I've taken personality tests, I always come back as a "quick start," which may just be a nice way of saying, "you're impulsive, you lack follow-through, and you're undisciplined." The good news for me and for you if you happen to fall into the same boat is that discipline is a choice. Follow-through can be a learned behavior. Being impulsive can be replaced by a new set of habits.

Flywheel Effect

Jim Collins talks about the "flywheel effect" in his book, *Good to Great: Why Some Companies Make the Leap . . . and Others Don't*. Collins and his team researched thousands of highly successful companies and found that one of the key abilities of all the great companies they studied was their ability to overcome a weakness through continuous improvement. The metaphor that Collins employs here is a flywheel. He writes:

> Picture a huge, heavy flywheel—a massive metal disk mounted horizontally on an axle, about 30 feet in diameter, 2 feet thick, and weighing about 5,000 pounds. Now imagine that your task is to get the flywheel rotating on the axle as fast and long as possible. Pushing with great effort, you get the flywheel to inch forward, moving almost imperceptibly at first. You keep pushing and, after two or three hours of persistent effort, you get the flywheel to complete one entire turn.

He goes on to write about how each turn of the flywheel builds upon work done earlier, and it eventually gains almost unstoppable momentum.

My tendency is to think about the breakthrough coming all at once, from some heroic, one-time act. However, if I've learned anything from Saban and Collins it is this: the daily, incremental, focused efforts are what lead to sustainable momentum and eventually breakthrough. It's easy to be amazed by the overnight successes, but what we often do not see are the years of effort that preceded the breakthrough.

One year I decided our flywheel was going to be operations. In full disclosure, this was not my favorite part of owning and running shops! But with steady, incremental effort we managed to get that flywheel moving at some pretty high speeds by year's end. Initially, though, it was just one turn at a time.

Your Scorecard

Finance was definitely my Achilles' heel in owning shops. After selling my shops in 2021, I've had a lot of time to reflect on what I would do differently. Getting a stronger understanding of business finance in general and a better grasp on my financials would likely be in the top three.

Here are a few things that I learned the hard way.

From my grandpa, I learned the old adage: "If you aim at nothing, you will certainly hit it." For many years I was flying blind. I had no idea what I was even aiming for. Instead, I would just land a repair, do the work, deliver it, and hope for the best. Then I would pay my bills as they came in. Often there was more month than money. I thought I could fix that with more sales. Turns out if you have holes in your pockets, no matter how much money you put in there it will just keep falling out! Growing sales was not the answer. The answer was in some advice my dad kept trying to teach me.

Dad told me over and over, "It's not what you make, it's what you keep!" I was making money. It just wasn't sticking around for long! In the process of trying to fix everything with sales, I learned a lot about how to make money. Keeping money was actually much harder to master.

What eventually tied it all together was having a scorecard that I held myself and my team accountable to. It's those KPIs—key performance indicators—that we hear so much about. At first, it all seemed so confusing. Which numbers were important? There was so much data coming at me from my accountant, from our estimating software, from insurance and rental car companies. I had to simplify it and get down to just a handful of measurables. At first, we had a weekly leadership meeting and our scorecard had twelve items on it. Eventually we landed on just a few that we measured weekly and a few that we measured monthly. Once you start working on it, you'll likely find as we did that less is more. Having just a handful of measures is not only easier, it's better and creates more cohesion and a focus for you and your team.

How Flying Made Me a Better Entrepreneur

I recall when my wife and kids bought me a "discovery flight" as a Father's Day gift. After years of loving motorcycles and cars and having adventures on road and off, they decided the next logical place to motor was up.

I still remember climbing into the cockpit of this small plane for the first time. After getting over the initial round of claustrophobia and reminding the pilot several times this was my first time in a small plane and I had a family and business to look after, we were ready for flight.

As we rolled down the runway at about 90 mph he said, "Now gently pull back on the yoke," and just like that, the plane lifted off the ground and we were flying. It was like riding a motorcycle or driving for the first time. All of the familiar feelings came rushing back.

I signed up for a few more lessons. Early on the most important thing I learned was the importance of keeping this order in mind:

1. aviate
2. navigate
3. communicate

One day at about five thousand feet, it dawned on me that these principles, ordered in this way, also apply to running a business:

1. Aviate: Do what is needed to keep things running.
2. Navigate: Know where you're going and steer the operation toward that goal.
3. Communicate: Check in with advisors who can make sure you get to where you're going intact.

As shop owners, it's easy to get stuck in the *aviate* part of our shops. We have to make payroll. We have to pay bills. In my case we had to get cars assigned to techs, then get them painted and delivered. We had to write estimates and supplements. We had to answer the phone and deal with customers and adjusters. These are some of the many kinds of daily tasks we cannot ignore if we want to keep "flying," as it were.

At some point, though, you develop systems and processes for many of these routine tasks so you're not constantly reinventing the wheel or overly focused on the day-to-day operations. Once these things are running relatively smoothly, it's time to *navigate*.

Where is your business going? Where do you want it go? Where are you right now in terms of financial performance?

What goals do you have for the upcoming month, quarter, year, or even the next five years?

These are the questions of navigation, and they can only be answered after some research and reflection. If you're wondering who has time for that, you are still focused on just flying. That's important, but navigation needs to be added into the sequence. First, we run our businesses, then we figure out where we want to take them and make sure we stay on course.

Finally, *communicating* is really important. In aviation, after you aviate, you then navigate, and you must communicate. You have to communicate to the people on the ground who can guide you to fly safely since they know where the other planes are in that area. They also help you land safely since they know what order the landings need to occur. They have the big picture and are communicating with several pilots at once.

Often entrepreneurs think others can read their minds. The tendency to undercommunicate is strong because typically we are thinking faster than we can remember to communicate. We're off to the next idea, assuming everyone understands how to execute on the last three assignments we gave them yesterday. We are focused on flying and setting direction. But if we don't communicate to our team, they can't help us achieve the things we see so clearly.

Leadership Development

Leaders often attempt to do one of two things: make people happy or drive them to perform. Those who can do both, win.

Having good leadership in your business is critical from the owner to those doing the daily work. But what is leadership? Often leadership feels like an idea or an ideal, but what does it look like in everyday situations? Someone once said, "Managers do things right. Leaders do the right thing."

Leadership is different than management in many ways, but one of the clearest is being able to chart a course for a team of people and not just follow a prescribed way of doing something. Leadership is more creative, fluid, and relational and therefore more difficult in many ways. With leadership, there are no pat answers, only fresh challenges that require creative thinking and bold action.

In my shops I always made an effort to develop managers into leaders. However, as the saying goes, "You can lead a horse to water but you can't make them drink." I found this to be so true, and despite my best efforts, resources, exposure to trainings, conversations, mentoring, hoping, etc., some managers just are not capable of making the leap to leadership. But those who are end up being happier personally and professionally. Learning to lead is not only a way to get higher profits; it also connects people to a higher purpose, better relationships, and greater respect in their wider circle of friends, family, and community.

So how do we become better leaders, and how do we develop those around us into leaders? While this can be difficult, it doesn't have to be overly complicated or confusing.

In 1945 there was a study done at Ohio State University in which researchers studied the performance of International Harvester foremen. What they found was that the most effective leaders exhibited two key behaviors. First, the best performers demonstrated consideration for those they led. In other words, they treated their employees with respect and dignity. They treated them like human beings, not cogs in a wheel to be used for their own professional progress. Second, the highest performers implemented disciplined structures and processes that moved their team members and the organization as a whole to higher performance.

From this study we can conclude that the two key behaviors for becoming an effective leader are simply demonstrating care for the people on your team and driving performance with a disciplined approach to implementing structure, systems, and processes. People skills. Performance skills. That's it. Simple? Yes. Easy? No.

The road to becoming a leader and developing leaders around you is never going to be easy because most people are naturally gifted on one side of that equation or the other. You either have a natural tendency toward people skills or performance skills; developing your weak side is the key to becoming a great leader.

Personally, I have always struggled on the performance skills side of that equation. I re-entered this industry after over fifteen years of social work and professional ministry. For obvious reasons, those professions lean heavily toward developing people skills like empathy, helpfulness, and service.

I've found that one of the best ways to develop your weak side is to find a high-leverage habit or behavior that can be practiced daily. A high-leverage action means if you can make progress on this one thing, several other things will come along with it. This is what Charles Duhigg calls a "keystone habit" in his book *The Power of Habit*.

An example from my personal life is exercise. When I make time to exercise, I automatically start to eat better, sleep better, and have more energy during the day, and my confidence improves. The same is true in our businesses. There are key behaviors—daily practices and habits that, once installed into our routines, will create positive momentum in several areas.

Here are some key behaviors to consider under each of those two categories—people skills and performance skills.

If you need to develop the *people skills* side of the equation, spend a little time each day interacting with each of your team members on a personal level. Find out what is important to them outside of work. Ask how their family is doing. Do they have any hobbies or things besides cars that occupy them outside of work? Ask questions and really listen to the answers. Often that means shutting up and waiting for a response before moving on or filling the silence with more words. And work on making eye contact when you're speaking to them. This demonstrates you are sincerely listening. Of course too much eye contact is creepy, but too little unintentionally communicates that you really don't care about what they're saying. If you are trying to develop people skills and you already know this is not your strong side, hold the eye contact a little longer than you would normally be comfortable with.

If, like me, you need to develop the *performance* side of the equation, spend time working on a key process your team keeps fumbling. For us at one point that was customer intake. When we were checking cars in, we would miss a step or two that seemed small but often would create problems down the line as the repair progressed. Our team often missed simple things like tagging the key, putting it on the roster, making sure there were pictures attached to the repair order, or writing key information on the car. I developed a checklist for whoever was doing the intake. There were about ten key things I wanted our receptionists to do before handing the job off to a manager, so I listed them in a checklist format, then printed off several copies and explained that every job had to be processed in this exact way.

So find a recurring problem, something that bugs you, that your team struggles with inexplicably, and turn it into a personal challenge to fix it with a new process that you develop and communicate to your team. Then hold them accountable to do it right every time, with excellence and precision.

Growing in our ability to lead and developing the leaders around us does not need to be complicated. But it has to be intentional. I am confident the results will be both surprising and rewarding.

It's All about the Questions

How do we help someone grow into a leader? The answer is in the questions. Here are some key questions that have stood the test of time and practice.

In his book *The Coaching Habit*, Michael Bungay Stanier says the single most effective question we can use to develop others is the "AWE question." AWE stands for "And what else?" This question is a great add-on after we have already asked another question, such as "What's on your mind?"

What typically happens after we ask a question is the person we're talking to will provide some surface-level answers. This is normal. But the AWE question can then be introduced to go deeper. "And what else have you been thinking about?" This encourages both deeper self-disclosure and more creative thinking. Stanier writes, "'And what else?' is the quickest and easiest way to uncover and create new possibilities."

Would you like to have more creative thinking about the areas where you feel stuck in your shop? Perhaps it's time to dig deeper into those issues by asking your team, "And what else?"

In her book *Fierce Conversations*, Susan Scott offers several questions that take people deeper quickly. These are the types of questions that will jump-start any meeting but are especially useful for one-on-one meetings with someone you are trying to develop into a leader. Here's a few she suggests that I found especially helpful:

- What's the most important thing we should be talking about today?
- What topic are you hoping I will not bring up?
- What is the most important decision you are facing?
- What is keeping you from making it?

Using these questions in meetings moves directly where you want to go with the leaders you are developing. They have a way of cutting through the fluff and getting to the heart of a matter quickly. As entrepreneurs we don't have a lot of time to waste on frivolous meetings. These questions are a beeline to the real conversations you need to have.

Finally, asking "why?" five times in a row helps get to the root cause of any issue. If the person you are mentoring is stuck or if a process in your business is stuck, you can start by asking, "Why are we stuck on this particular problem?" The answer to that question, if based on facts, will then lead you to another round of asking, "Well, why is that the case?" If you persistently and honestly dig down on any issue with five *why*s, chances are good you will arrive at a root cause. And once a root cause is discovered, solutions will quickly follow.

When we are mentoring someone, our knee-jerk reaction will be to offer solutions. It is simply how we are wired. We are fixers! We want to give solutions, be the hero, and really help people move past their sticking points. The only problem with that is they will never learn to think on their own, solve their own problems, and become leaders. Fixing things for people is the surest way to lock them into being followers, not leaders. And ultimately those with real leadership ability will resent you for it.

People need to be empowered to solve their own problems and come up with their own strategies. We must learn to become guides, not fixers, and our greatest tools are questions.

Meaningful Meetings

A great tool that helped us thrive in this stage is meetings. Now if you're like me, you did not become the owner of a small business because you just love meetings. Almost no one loves meetings. But is that the meetings' fault? The antidote to bad meetings is good meetings, not no meetings.

Meetings, if done right, have great power and can move the needle on getting things done. They can build teamwork and reinforce culture. Meetings—good meetings—are essential to moving us closer to our vision of having a thriving business and building a resilient legacy.

So how do we go from meaningless to meaningful meetings? By being clear on why they are needed and having a clear agenda and outcomes for each one.

When our shop grew to two locations, we began having more meetings than we used to. In order to coordinate between the shops and also because of my role, I began attending similar meetings at two different locations as well as meetings to coordinate efforts between the shops. Thankfully, I was not leading all the meetings, as I had some very capable leaders on my team. Eventually I attended fewer meetings as they got traction and took on a life of their own.

Here are the types of meetings we regularly had:

Production meetings: A daily meeting of the managers, estimators, and parts manager at each location to go over all jobs and talk about what's next on each. These meetings also prepared us as a team to update our customers. We took notes on every job's status and what was next on a centralized spreadsheet so that anyone could update a customer who called.

Leadership teams: Each week the leadership teams at each location met to discuss some of the important but not urgent items. This meeting tended to blend some of the strategic goals but with a stronger emphasis on the tactical. For instance, a strategic goal might be to improve cycle time and then we would brainstorm together the tactics to achieve that or dig into a few actual jobs to see how we could have done better.

OSM: This is an acronym for "Operation Smart Money." When I hired a controller, someone who was like an in-house accountant, we decided we needed to meet weekly to discuss how to optimize profits. This was morphing into my executive team that oversaw the strategy for both shops. It was made up of my controller, director of operations, chief financial officer (CFO), and me.

Shop lunches: This was a monthly meeting for the teams of each location to share a meal in the shop and was also the primary place where we built culture. We usually catered in a meal. Once we did a chili cook-off for which four team members volunteered to make chili and then we voted on the best one. As previously discussed, we also did "atta boys" and "atta girls" at the shop lunches where team members got to brag about colleagues going above and beyond during that particular month. We started by going around the table and everyone shared a bit of good news that was happening in their personal life. We also read a recent positive online review.

Department lunches: The general manager from each location had a budget to take one department each week out to lunch and just check in and say thanks for what they did for the wider team.

One-to-ones: Each week I personally did a one-to-one lunch or coffee with a manager as part of their personal development and again as a way to encourage them and thank them for their unique contribution to the team.

Even just listing all those meetings feels draining! What I came to discover, though, was how much actually got done in those meetings that could not have happened any other way.

For instance, there's no way we would have had the culture we grew without the monthly shop lunches. When those started it was hard to get anyone to talk. Most of the team did not even want to be there. But over time people started to open up and learned to both receive and give praise for a job well done. It was also a key time for us to share for a few minutes one of our core values, like customer service, generosity, or quality craftsmanship.

What can you do to foster more meaningful meetings?

The first thing is to review the meetings you have and make sure there's a clear purpose for them. What is the meeting intended to accomplish? Then be brutally honest and ask if it is actually accomplishing that.

Second is to have an agenda for each meeting prepared ahead of time if possible, or at least at the start of the meeting. Then set an end time, with an alarm, for the meeting and move through the agenda from the most important and pressing topic to the least. Sounds obvious and easy, but in practice this takes a lot of skill. As I have noted, for one-on-one meetings I like to use a question I learned from Susan Scott in her book *Fierce Conversations* to set the agenda: "What is the most important thing we need to talk about today?"

Third, make room for the various personality types in the meeting. Extroverts will help get a conversation going but will also happily dominate meetings, whereas introverts may have something really crucial to add but will gladly sit on it rather than put it out there. This may mean calling on a quieter team member with a gentle, "You look like you may have something to add here," and giving time and space for them to share or the freedom not to if they're not ready.

Lastly, make a list of to-dos that are needed and who is going to do them—decisions that were made even if no action is required right away. And list any changes of direction that were agreed on.

What Can Happen, Part 1

One week, we blew one of our daily goals out of the water. And what excited me the most had nothing at all to do with the fact that we surpassed a goal. We had a daily goal in our shop to deliver six cars each day, Monday through Friday. I wanted that to become the average, normal day. One Friday, we delivered seventeen cars and had three more ready that could have gone, though the customers were not able to pick them up for various reasons.

Now I know for other shops this is not a lot and perhaps delivering twenty cars is just an average day. For others, delivering six in a day might feel like a dream. For us, getting twenty cars through our detail department in one day was a massive feat. Many of the deliveries had just been painted and reassembled that very day. To do three times the number of cars on a single day was breakthrough work on my team's part.

But again, that is not what excited me the most. What really impressed me was when I went around at the end of the day to thank the team for their extraordinary efforts, they all started pointing at other team members and gave them the credit.

I started in our detail department and gave one of our detailers a high five and a "way to go!" The first thing out of his mouth was, "We couldn't have done this today without paint doing such a great job this week on keeping the paint jobs as clean as we've ever seen them. I don't know what they did, but they should get the credit because we hardly had to buff at all."

I thought that was interesting, as detail had been complaining for weeks about overspray and how dirty the paint jobs were and how much extra work it had been at the end to get cars ready for delivery. Hmmm. Next I sent a text to a manager and thanked him for organizing the cars in such a way that we were able to get that many delivered. He immediately said, "Honestly, Andrew did that."

I texted back, "How's that even possible? He wasn't even here today!"

"Well, he did such a good job earlier in the week it made today seem easy," the manager said. "All those cars were already on a fast track to detail before he left yesterday."

And on it went. Department by department. Every time I thanked someone for their efforts, they immediately credited someone else.

This is literally the stuff my dreams are made of! I knew each person I thanked had a huge hand in pulling off that many deliveries. But they deflected the praise and pointed at someone else.

And just so we're clear: This was not a normal part of our team's culture. There were plenty of seasons when my team felt very underappreciated and there was conflict between departments. However, this day needed to be remembered and marked as a major breakthrough, not just in productivity but more importantly as a win for our culture.

Jim Collins in his outstanding book, *Good to Great*, talks about level 5 leaders as the most effective leaders. One of the core traits of a level 5 leader is their ability to take the blame for their team's failures and to credit their team for the wins.

Jim uses the images of a mirror and a window. Lower-level leaders look in the mirror when it's time to assign credit for the wins and out the window to blame others when there's a loss. Level 5 leaders do the opposite and look in the mirror when the team fails and ask the really hard questions about what part they may have played in that failure. Then, after a win, they look out the window to see who they can give the credit to, even when they had a huge part to play in achieving the win.

For several days after this big delivery day, I was asking myself, "How did we turn the corner on getting our team to credit others for the wins we are currently experiencing?"

What kept coming to me was our shop lunches. Once a month, we gathered our team in the shop for a meal. We shut the shop down for an hour and spent that time eating together and talking about our goals and how we're doing against them. But the part that seemed to finally be starting to stick was the "atta boys" and "atta girls" we did.

At first this was just about the managers finding a few team members who demonstrated extra effort in some way over the course of the month and singling them out with a short word of praise and a small gift card of some kind. But then we started having the team do the "atta boys" or "atta girls" for each other. The first few times we did this there was very little response. But about a month prior to this breakthrough day, the managers noted how this praise time became the longest part of the lunch meeting, as there were so many people wanting to make sure their coworkers were getting the credit they deserved. Every time we started to cut it off, another hand would shoot up in the air and we'd do "just one more."

The best part for me was how this practice of encouraging went from something we did at a shop meeting that felt kind of uncomfortable, and at times even a bit forced, to now being just a normal part of our day.

What Can Happen, Part 2

Since exiting the body shop business, I have focused attention on building our family business of short-term rentals. At a recent family meeting, my son was stuck on a marketing challenge. He had set a goal of getting to a thousand followers on social media, especially our business's Facebook page. But we kept bouncing off the ceiling at about 750.

He knew this was an important goal for our marketing, that it would drive more sales as each follower represented not just one person as a potential guest in one of our short-term rentals but their whole network as well. He knew we could leverage each and every one of those relationships to build our fledgling enterprise. But he was stuck.

So one of my daughters suggested that we set the rest of the meeting agenda aside for a few minutes and work on this issue together as a team to see if we could unlock it together. We brainstormed a short list of ideas that might work then picked the top one that we agreed had the most potential. And voila! Right there in the meeting we unlocked it. We remembered that there was a way to invite all your friends at one time. We couldn't remember the specifics, but that was quickly resolved with a two-minute search online. It was as simple as my son making me and my daughter admins of the page along with him, and then we were able to invite our networks to become friends and followers and fans of the page. So we did that and then got back to our meeting. By the time the meeting was over we had already jumped from 750 to 850 followers on the page. We were elated! It looked like that challenge was solved with a small amount of teamwork in a very short time.

More than the actual result, it raised our confidence that these meetings are not wasted time going in circles but can actually produce real results toward meaningful goals and outcomes.

Play It Right, Then Different

There's a saying in jazz: First you learn to play it right, then you learn to play it different. Or think about painters. They are constrained by the canvas. These constraints, these controls are the very things that allow them to focus their creativity.

Creating controls and boundaries via checklists, a defined playbook, having consistently good meetings, and developing other leaders are the boundary conditions of doing great, creative work.

One last point: None of this sacred! If you as the entrepreneur want to improve or change a process because you've discovered a better way, go for it! That's where your creativity comes in! As long as you are building on the foundations already set via controls, the later versions of a system or process will be better than the original.

Play it right. *Then* play it different.

6

PROSPERITY

Owning an Asset, Not a Job

LET ME PAINT a picture for you.

You have cast your corporate vision. You have given direction to everyone involved. You have a big ten-year goal that cascades all the way down to three-year, one-year, and quarterly goals.

You have clearly communicated your core values. Everyone knows how they are to behave en route to these goals with the values as their guardrails. Your values have solidified into a culture that gets reinforced as each person continues to move and live in this wonderful ecosystem you and your staff have created.

The operations are solid with a clear playbook, job descriptions, and checklists for all the major tasks. Your PnL is showing solid growth and throwing off cash.

What would it look like for you to be able to walk away from your business and have it keep running without you and actually thrive, grow even, and continue to pay you? What would have to be true for that to happen?

When you can figure this out and implement it, you're on your way to the prosperity stage.

The Way to Prosperity

To succeed, it's important to find ways to work *on* your business, not just *in* it. In other words, the prosperous business owner differentiates from their business. You are not your business, and your business is not you. Your business does not determine your ultimate worth or success. But what it allows you to do through its success can be used to do things that really matter—like family vacations and time to work on your spiritual life.

One of my first business mentors told me, "Your business should be a cash cow. It should pay you well whether you're there or not. In fact, as time goes on, you will be investing less and less time and effort in your business, but it will be making you more and more money." I just sat there stunned. I had never been told this before, and frankly it did not compute.

At the time I was living with a much simpler formula in mind: your time + your effort = money. To make more money meant you had to work more. It was a very "industrial revolution" way to think about work.

A more advantageous metaphor might be farming. Farmers work very hard. But they work in a way that compounds their efforts over time. Once a field is cleared and plowed, it doesn't require the same amount of effort the next year to prepare and plow. So they can actually get more done in the same amount of time and effort the next year. We can see how this could quickly compound by years three, four, five, and so on.

Another way to think about this is the power of tools. Imagine you are tasked with digging a ditch that is ten feet deep. You're handed a shovel. Now imagine that same task but you're given a bulldozer. Man is a tool-making animal.

Since the beginning of time, we have made tools to aid and multiply our efforts.

So perhaps a new formula is needed. We may need to change the formula from

$$\text{time} + \text{effort} = \text{profit}$$

to

$$\text{time} + \text{leveraged effort} = \text{prosperity}$$

That leveraged effort can come in the form of repeatable and predictable processes, people on your team functioning at their highest and best, or even just a new tool.

The goal is to create an enterprise that gives you more time and money. How you get that time and money can come through selling or just letting it run without your direct involvement.

Five Steps to a Month-Long Sabbatical

I began writing this book while I was still running the auto body shops. And this section was written in Bonavista, Newfoundland, Canada, on the tail end of a month-long trip away. It's beautiful there! It's the kind of beauty that restores the soul. Wide-open ocean views, sunsets that seem to never end, and getting up close with enormous humpback whales. The pace of life there is slower, with lots of room to breathe and take long walks. More importantly, my wife and I were able to connect with extended family over meals and adventures.

Some of you might be saying, "Hold up! Did you just say you took a month-long vacation? How?"

That's a fair question! Most of us lead or manage our businesses, and the thought of taking a month off seems not only crazy but impossible. I totally get that. There was definitely a time when it would not have been possible for me either. There are seasons in a business that simply require the owner to be fully present. In the early days when I was the estimator, bookkeeper, and production and parts manager, there's no way I could be gone for a month. Not a chance!

But as the business grew and I was able to hire people who were literally better than me at every single aspect of my business, I was freer to be away. Some things still couldn't be delegated. As the owner I had to set the goals and pace of the organization. I had to make sure our values were upheld and the culture stayed on track. I was the only person who could decide on the biggest issues, like which shops we want to acquire and our higher purpose. I still had a job to do, but I wasn't really needed for the day-to-day.

Do you want to be able to take a month-long sabbatical? It really is possible. It all comes down to five factors.

First, culture. Culture creates freedom. With your values clearly communicated and a team that can refer to these values, decision-making becomes easier.

Second, a trusted team. If you hire talented people who are better than you at specific tasks, pay them well, and encourage them, they will gladly take care of your business while you're away. I have a friend whose father gave him this advice: "Hire the best people you can, and pay them as much as you can." You get what you pay for. If you want to save a few bucks by hiring people of lower skill to run your shop or do your bookkeeping or greet your customers, well, you will likely pay for that in other ways! Of course there are limits here, but make sure you are at the higher end of the pay scale to attract the kind of people who can run your shop as well as you can.

Third, at least for some, joining a franchise or a network of businesses cooperating in the same industry. By joining the

CARSTAR franchise we found other people who helped me keep an eye on things in the business. One of the questions I get asked most often about joining a franchise is, "Do they dictate how you run your business?" I can honestly say, not in the least. They were there to coach and offer input as needed. And they had a vested interest in making sure my shops ran profitably so they got their fees, maintained their insurance relationships, and preserved the reputation of the wider network. Our interests were aligned. I wanted those same things! It was helpful—and quite honestly, comforting—to have others checking on the health of my shops for me and offering feedback as needed.

Fourth, connectivity. There were several days during my vacation when I was interrupted out of necessity. We were right in the middle of acquiring more locations. Decisions needed to be made. Investors and banks needed information. Some discussions with sellers simply couldn't wait. In those situations, even though I was three hours from the nearest airport, my phone and email worked. I've learned that a lot can get done with these simple tools! Thankfully I wasn't needed every day, but it was good to be connected when I absolutely had to be involved.

Lastly, sufficient size. Referring to the auto repair business, many shop owners I've talked to are afraid to scale because of all the extra work that involves. The assumption is that taking on a second or third shop means two times the work, and there just aren't enough hours in the week when they do that simple math. I believe, however, not scaling actually ties owners to their business in ways that don't apply to those who choose to scale.

For instance, as we grew, I had the resources to hire people to do all the tasks I wasn't very good at anyway. We all have those tasks that simply drain us. As I've mentioned, bookkeeping and accounting are not my jam. I could not wait to get those tasks off my plate in the early days. Now I have a whole team of people, including bookkeepers, at each shop as well as a controller who manages cash flow across all the locations and interacts with my accountant as needed.

I have a friend who used to own more than ten shops. He told me, "The hardest thing I ever did in my whole career was own and run two shops. The easiest thing I ever did was own and operate eight." Scale comes with advantages, and one of the biggest is freedom to do the tasks you are really good at and enjoy. This makes your time at work more enjoyable and getting away that much easier.

Culture: Scaling Your Vision and Values

What is at the core of your company culture? What have you decided to be for or against? What values are guiding your business into the future?

Even though my first love in business is marketing, I have found myself reflecting repeatedly on bigger questions of leadership, culture, and values. When my shop had its ten-year anniversary, something about that big, round number captured my imagination. It seemed like a good time to reflect back on the progress we had made and the challenges ahead—and plan for the years to come.

We decided to put generosity at the core of our business, and the story below is part of the fabric of why we chose this value to guide our culture.

Several years ago, my family traveled to Guatemala to visit some missionary friends. While there, we had some of the most amazing experiences of our lives. We hiked up an active volcano that literally burned the soles of our shoes the higher we climbed. We came within a few feet of red-hot lava! We shopped in Antigua, a beautiful colonial-style city with old cathedrals and street vendors.

But the most beautiful place we visited was easily Lake Atitlan, a place philosopher Aldous Huxley called the most beautiful place on earth. Imagine deep blue waters surrounded on all sides by soaring volcanic mountains. It's a remarkable place.

We also got to see the results of our friends' work in the poorest slum in all of Central America, a place called La Limonada, which has a river of sewage running right through the middle of it. This shantytown is riddled with gang violence, drugs, untreated illnesses, trash, and poorly constructed "homes" often made of cardboard and other discarded materials.

My friends worked at a school with children who face the most abject poverty every day. The school is about much more than education. It also feeds two meals each day, provides clothes, and teaches basic hygiene.

The school impressed us, especially the staff, who live very sacrificially so these kids can have a chance to escape the cycle of poverty most of them would be stuck in otherwise. The staff is made up mostly of Guatemalans, who themselves grew up in this neighborhood, supplemented by some teachers and helpers who come from other places including the United States.

While there, my wife and I discovered most of the staff had never been to Lake Atitlan, even though it was only a short drive away. Why? They couldn't afford it. When we got home, my wife and I did some research and discovered that for $2,000, the whole school staff (more than twenty people) and all of the helpers could get to Lake Atitlan and have food and lodging covered. It was a no-brainer. We had to do this.

The following Christmas, we sent the school $2,000 as a gift from our shop, so the staff could have a long weekend away to rejuvenate at Lake Atitlan. The staff sent us thank-you letters afterward expressing how much they needed the break and how much it meant to them to get away and see this beautiful place. It brought us to tears that such a small gift could mean so much.

This was a great experience, but the challenge was to translate this deep value of generosity to the rest of my team at the auto body shop. It finally dawned on me that one key way to instill this into our shop culture was to get them involved in giving. I decided to do matching grants to any employee who gave money to a nonprofit of their choosing. The shop matched it up to $250. This way, the generosity started with them but linked to the shop and their daily work.

It would be hard to argue against generosity as an important value for any shop to have. But does it really make good business sense? The business value can be summarized by one word: engagement. You will find a more engaged workforce and more engaged customers. Team members will start to sense they are part of something bigger than themselves and even bigger than your shop. It adds a larger sense of contribution and purpose.

What part of your culture are you working on, and how do you help employees align with your values? Intentionally developing your culture so that it pervades your work place even when you're gone is a key element to scaling your business and being able to remove yourself from the day-to-day.

What Does Prosperity Look Like?

What is prosperity? There is the prosperity gospel that seems like it is a distortion of the gospel. It's very transactional. If I do X (give enough, pray enough, fast enough, evangelize enough), God will reward me twofold or fivefold or whatever.

This message draws some people, but so many Christians run the other way!

For some Christians, poverty is the ideal. Money is suspect, and those who really succeed must have cheated the system or done something unscrupulous. While I do believe some are called to radical simplicity and on rare occasions even poverty, the promise of prospering in this life and the life to come runs all through Scripture.

- "The plans of the diligent lead to profit" (Proverbs 21:5 NIV).
- "The LORD...has pleasure in the prosperity of his servants" (Psalm 35:27 NKJV).
- "Then the LORD your God will make you most prosperous in all the work of your hands.... The Lord will again delight in you and make you prosperous" (Deuteronomy 30:9 NIV).

Luke 2:52, for example, says Christ "grew in *wisdom* and *stature*, and in favor with *God* and *man*" (NIV). Note what I've italicized: wisdom, stature, God, and man. Those are four areas of life: intellectual, physical, spiritual, and relational. What if we took these four areas and asked, "What would it look like to prosper in each?"

Then ask, "What would having the time and money to invest deeply in each of these areas mean for me?" Whatever your answer is to this question is true prosperity for you. Prosperity is having the time and resources to invest in ourselves, in others (our families for starters), and in things that matter to us (causes).

Imagine that your business is really prospering. It's throwing off good cash reliably, and it doesn't require an inordinate amount of your time. You have freedom of time and money.

You are investing well outside your business. You have savings and a fully funded emergency fund. You're being generous to your local church and several causes that have deep meaning to you. You can now start to think about what to do with that extra money.

You could invest it in your intellectual life by taking a class or two that might interest you. Or how about your relational life? You could take your spouse on that vacation that you've always talked about and create a lifetime of memories! Or what about that son or daughter trip you've always wanted to do! The possibilities are endless.

For me it was motorcycle trips with my son and the aforementioned month-long sabbatical to where my wife's family lives in Newfoundland, Canada, complete with whale watching, four-wheeling, fishing with my daughter, and fresh-caught lobster dinners with our extended family.

Different Ways to Use Wealth

Now I want to suggest, very briefly, some ways to use our wealth, our financial capital, to up our game in other areas:

- Physical capital: We can have time to work out and afford a gym membership or even a trainer. We can shop for and eat healthier foods.
- Mental capital: We can afford to get training. Buy books, especially audible ones. Buy subscriptions to book summary services. We can contribute to an education fund for our kids and grandkids. We have time to write books—the book you're reading is part of my legacy—or even just a series of emails or journals to leave with descendants, sharing wisdom gained over a lifetime.

- Relational capital: We can afford the family vacations. We can afford to do things with our kids and grandkids that build memories. We can leave money for our grandchildren's education.
- Spiritual capital: We will have time to invest in our church's ministries. We will have freedom to go on retreats and to conferences. We are able to leave a legacy through generosity to churches and nonprofits.
- Financial capital: We can give gifts that keep on giving—for example, endowments that throw off interest that can be used for education and nonprofits.

You Don't Have to Wait

Of course many of these things can be worked into your life right now. For instance, perhaps you can't afford the expensive gym and trainer right now. But you can take walks in nature, stretch, and get adequate rest. All that is free. Likewise, you may not be able to afford an advanced degree or travel to an interesting place to learn a new skill. But you can likely afford to buy great books or go to a library and absorb the best thinking out there on almost any challenge you're currently facing.

Also, remember God does not waste opportunities to shape you in the context of your business. When things get hard or confusing or downright overwhelming, God is there, shaping you, helping you, guiding you. Most of all God is inviting you to welcome him in, to ask for his help. God wants to be a part of all that. It's not bothering him if you ask for help! He has an endless supply of wisdom, energy, and time at his disposal. But we do have to ask.

We have to humble ourselves enough to say to him "I need help!" But he will be there. Not visibly. And not always in the timing you want. He is patient and not in a hurry. And not always in the way you expect. He likes to surprise us and often has many more creative answers than we could ever imagine.

If you're not yet in the prosperous stage, be patient about growing your business, but be impatient about your own self-improvement.

Leaving a Legacy

I had dinner recently with a friend who knew someone who sold his company for over $600 million. That's a lot of zeros, and most people reading this book will not leave that kind of financial legacy. Yet shortly after he died his heirs who each inherited over $100 million began to fight over his estate! This is the shadow side of leaving a legacy without imparting wisdom and virtue.

Imagine having over $100 million being passed on to you all at once, and the first thing you do is quibble over thousands. Who cares! What's even a million here or there at that level!

This is why I began this book with the idea of virtue. If you become a virtuous and wise person over the course of your life, you win. As Christians we understand that this life is not our ultimate destiny. Scripture calls this life "grass" and a "wisp of smoke" (Psalm 103:15, James 4:14). It's not that it's unimportant, but it's not the whole story.

This life is mostly about who we become. If we can attain even some measure of virtue—love, faith, hope, patience, kindness, humility, and contentment—we have done all that has been asked of us. If we can pass those virtues and wisdom on to our descendants—our children and those we influence and mentor—we have won big! If we can learn virtue, help others attain virtue, and leave a financial inheritance that scales values like generosity, justice, love, and kindness and keep them flowing forward in time, well, we've hit the jackpot of life's purpose.

7
LEGACY
Outliving Your Earthly Days

AT THIS POINT we've come through all the stages of gaining competence. We started by not even knowing what we didn't know. We then descended into the most painful stage of learning, discovering all the things we don't know. With time, patience, mentors, and many other means, we somehow managed to come out of the pit of dread and chaos.

We eventually got to the place of knowing what we know. At this stage it wasn't effortless. There was still a lot of work to do in setting up the systems and personnel to make it to that higher stage when things would be just as productive with a lot less effort.

At some point we got to the point where our systems and people and processes and even our revenue became automatic, at times effortless. We were living in a prosperous time where the business was functioning equally well with or without our direct efforts. We were free to dream again, to set the course for the next season. We were free to plan for things that were one, three, or even five years out. Our cash flow became more predictable.

This is the season when it's time to start asking questions like:

- Do we scale this?
- Do we sell this?
- Do we let it run and provide us predictable cash flow?

No matter which path you choose, you now have the ability to focus on legacy and living for the next generation.

Legacy for the Christian entrepreneur is where it all comes together. This is when you focus on a really big future that will outlive your earthly days via your descendants, both family and those you mentor.

My Decision to Sell

At the end of 2021, after eighteen years of owning a shop that grew into five shops spread out over two states, I sold all my businesses but retained some of the real estate. This sale happened after almost eighteen years to the day, as I launched November 2003 and sold November 2021.

I wanted to sell while we were on an upswing.

We had just come through COVID, and like many family businesses it was a slog. We had to lay some people off. Work flow slowed down quite a bit. All the supply chain issues for getting parts made keeping customers happy that much harder. But we made it.

I hired a COO who had been a part of other multishop operations and had even worked briefly for a very large, billion-dollar consolidator. He had the chops to run multiple shops. Not just in theory; he had done it before. He helped get everything tightened up and pointed in the right direction with our PnL and our operations. That's when a hundred-shop group came knocking. We opened the door to discussions and ultimately said yes, we would sell.

The decision was relatively easy for me. I know I let some people down when I did this; however, I was losing my passion for the industry. Plus, I was ill-equipped to lead an organization of this size and magnitude. Sure, I could learn how. But with the passion draining I decided it was likely better to disappoint some people than force them to work with a passionless leader.

The Doldrums of Winning

After selling my business I experienced some mild depression. At first I didn't talk about it for the same reason I didn't talk about how much I owed in taxes. The only way to owe a lot in taxes is if you've made a lot of money to owe taxes on. In a sense, then, complaining about taxes is almost like you're complaining about how much money you made.

At some point, though, I started talking to other business owners and CEOs who had exited their businesses. And to a person they all shared my experience of having a period of mild depression. It's likely true that anyone who goes through a big win ends up feeling a sense of loss because the hunt to win is over.

This happens in other disciplines as well. Adam Peaty, an English swimmer who won the gold medal in the 100-meter breaststroke in the 2016 Olympics, said, "I experienced really bad post-Olympics blues after Rio. I went through that big lull of feeling lost, I didn't know what to do with myself; I'd achieved my absolute dream and Rio was the time of my life, but no one prepares you for what happens afterwards." I could relate to that even though my breaststroke is pretty weak.

It felt like my purpose was gone. I was trying to build something big enough to sell or go on autopilot, and I did it. It wasn't always straight up and to the right. There were setbacks. There were hardships. There were moments when it looked like it wasn't going to happen. But in all that doubt and turmoil there was a fight. There was a goal. There was a massive purpose with no guaranteed outcome of success. There was risk. There were obstacles. There were things I needed to learn and overcome, skills to develop that initially I didn't have. There were so many things to figure out with no guaranteed outcomes. There was uncertainty. All this contributed to feeling like I was part of something undetermined but exciting.

A New Realization

Overnight my focus shifted from worrying over my immediate finances to thinking about my children and their children. This was also when my first grandchild arrived, so that may have had something to do with it! But suddenly the word *legacy* kept presenting itself to me over and over.

Over the course of eighteen years, we had grown from one tiny shop doing $20 thousand per month to five shops doing $1 million in revenue per month. It had been an exhilarating ride! But when I sold all the shops, I knew I was set.

I didn't have any need or desire to change my lifestyle. Sure, I considered buying some fun new toys, but I held off. Several years later my wife and I were still driving the same cars. And we lived in the same house.

We were able to pay off all our debt, both personal and business. We retained ownership of the buildings that a couple of the shops operated out of, which provided good monthly income for us. We invested in other real estate. We developed a piece of property that we bought very inexpensively with some friends into a short-term rental business that our son still runs. And from one of the shops, we were getting a three-year payout. This gave us some time to let our investment properties mature into more passive income streams.

I came to realize I was finally able to live for the next generation in my family.

From Retiring to "Re-Tiring"

As we were wrapping up the sale of my businesses as well as coming to the end of a year, I was personally wrapping up my first year in a group coaching cohort. During one of our final sessions of the year, the facilitator announced we were going to do a "Word of the Year" exercise to help us nail down a theme for the upcoming year.

I have many friends who do this every year, and I've experimented with it a few times. However, I always felt like it was a little too constricting. How could you possibly have one word that would be a theme for something as varied and complex and unknown as a full year that has not been lived yet?

I had no idea how this was going to go. But as we got into the exercise it seemed like the heavens opened and a word just got dropped and planted in my heart. The word: legacy.

I was finally in a place after the sale where I had the resources and time to do pretty much whatever I wanted. I could have retired. Instead, God was calling me to "re-tire." One of my favorite things is riding motorcycles. I've loved it since I was a little kid on a mini bike and then shortly after getting a motorcycle that was much too big for me that I had to grow into. I remember lowering the forks all the way down in the first year just so my feet could touch the ground! To this day I love riding and especially riding off road. So when I heard the word "re-tire" in a new way, it made perfect sense. I was putting a fresh set of tires on for a new adventure. Nothing could have made me more excited!

Retirement sounds boring, scary even. My grandfather who retired died a week after retirement, so retirement has always had a very negative connotation for me. However, re-tiring? That's right up my alley! It seemed like the Lord wasn't done with me yet, and we were about to embark on a grand new adventure. I couldn't wait. And "legacy" was going to be my guiding motivation. This leg of the journey was less about me and "making it" and much more about what I will leave behind to my kids, grandkids, and future generations. So I began brainstorming.

Financially I wanted to invest the proceeds from the sale really well. I wanted to buy assets that will appreciate, not liabilities that will drain the abundance I just received.

Relationally I wanted to invest in making memories with those I care about most. Sure, I could have spent money on things that my wife and kids would have enjoyed, but what if I invested in real estate that would appreciate in value over time and be a blast to visit together? That's a win-win!

Physically I wanted to live for many, many years. I'm not afraid to die. I'm confident in what lies ahead for me, but I also wanted to be "in the land of the living" for as long as possible. In the Orthodox Church we sing a song called "Many Years" on a person's birthday. There is great value and blessing in living many years on this earth if you know how to live well.

I wanted to invest spiritually in my granddaughter's faith by starting to pray with her. I wanted to light candles with her, as I had done with my children, declaring Jesus is the light of the world, and say ancient prayers together that have stood the test of centuries and would most certainly be sturdy enough for her to use her whole life.

It All Comes Back to Family

For whatever reason I really like reality TV shows that involve competition. *Survivor. Master Chef. The Voice.* One thing I've observed over and over across all the different types of shows, whether singing, cooking, or survival, is that invariably the contestants talk about how their motivation to do the show and win is related to their family.

They had a dad who used to sing with them. They have a child to whom they want to demonstrate what a strong woman looks like. They were adopted and are using this experience to publicly express gratitude to their adopted parents. This often gets reinforced as the shows do little bits about the contestant's family. Or when the emcee announces who made the cut, which often is followed by a clip of the family celebrating far off. Some shows even have hometown homecomings that bring the remaining few contestants back to their homes so they can receive a hero's welcome and spend some time with their families.

Family seems to be the most natural and biggest *why* for most people. Even though as teenagers we may have tried to get away from our families, and even though we almost universally recognize that our families are flawed, it typically comes back to family. Some people have very tragic family lives with ties that are broken by abuse or neglect. Yet even they set off to create the family they never had.

Legacy has a lot to do with family.

But what about those with no family or people outside our immediate family whom we come to see as family. Our descendants are often more than our immediate family. Those we are mentored by and those we mentor often end up in our "family." I think of Jesus, who did not marry and have children, nor did any of the apostles as far as we know. And yet their families, spiritually speaking, were (and are) vast.

One17

Not long after selling our businesses, our family took the reins of a small foundation dedicated to funding adoption stories called One17 Foundation. It was named after the verse in Isaiah 1:17 where it says, "Learn to do right; seek justice. Defend the oppressed. Take up the cause of the fatherless; plead the case of the widow" (NIV).

My wife Tracy had been on the board of directors for this organization nearly since the beginning. The people who founded it were dear friends who had helped us with the adoption of our Colombian daughter. They introduced us to her and the staff of the orphanage where she lived. They helped us find the people in Colombia who walked us through the process. And they hosted a large fundraiser including a silent auction to raise money for the required two-month stay in Colombia while finalizing the adoption.

One17's mission aligns perfectly with our family's values of hospitality, generosity, and justice. Adoption is perhaps the highest form of hospitality, as you are not only welcoming someone into your home but into your family. Generosity is also at the core of One17, as people give to a fund that is disbursed to adoptive families nearing the final stages of welcoming a child into their home. Justice is on full display too, as children who might otherwise grow up in poverty now have a family and home life with loving parents and much greater stability and opportunity than they might otherwise have known.

Adoption has deeply influenced our family's story and will be a big part of our legacy. Not only did our youngest daughter join our family through adoption, the impact multiplies through our work with One17, which empowers more families to adopt and share their inspiring journeys, creating a ripple effect of change and connection.

Balancing Pleasure and Purpose

A big part of having a meaningful end of your career is learning to calibrate pleasure and purpose. I have several friends who are financial advisors, and they are regularly helping people who are retiring and trying to figure out what their golden years will look like.

Some people have the notion that retirement should be nothing but golfing, beaches, fishing (or plug in the hobby of your choice here). But what tends to happen is boredom can set in. We aren't designed to be engaged in endless hobbies!

Swinging too far the other way, we retirees can think that this season is all about finally getting to all those purposeful pursuits. For years perhaps they have looked at people like Mother Teresa and they think: This is the season to champion a cause. And before they know it they are on several nonprofit boards, helping out local soup kitchens or tutoring kids in underprivileged neighborhoods. But swinging too far that way can lead to burn out.

After I sold the shops, I had lunch with my friend, financial advisor James Lenhoff, who has seen many people in retirement swing too far to the extremes. He encouraged me to find the balance between the two. The challenge is to learn how to calibrate both purpose and pleasure.

Success *and* Significance

If the vast majority of our needs are met, we can call that success. We've made it. We may not have the lifestyle we want, but our basic needs are met. We are not wondering where our next meal is coming from, and we have at least a handful of meaningful relationships. For the more ambitious among us, we may feel we have a lot of room to achieve, but we are not vulnerable to our most basic needs going unmet.

What does it mean to go from success to lasting significance? I propose there are three facets of success.

First, looking outward beyond ourselves. As John Maxwell says, success is when I add value to myself. Significance is when I add value to others. Now don't get me wrong, it's important to care for our needs and our family's needs. It's like when the flight attendant tells us, in the event of an emergency, put the oxygen mask on ourselves before our children. It may seem counterintuitive, at first, to not care for our children, but making sure we have oxygen is the most important thing we can do at that moment. It's not selfish. It's critical so that we can care for our loved ones. The same is true with money. We care for our needs so that we can care better for others. We can't give what we don't have. But once we've met our own needs, the first step toward significance is investing in others.

Second, and very much related to the first, is to be generous. My friend Brian, who is the leader of a large nonprofit, often says, "You will never need to wonder if your life was meaningful if you've been generous to help truly vulnerable people." Generosity answers one of the biggest questions most people ask over the course of their lives, especially near the end: "Did my life matter?" If you've been generous, especially to the most vulnerable, you can confidently say, "Yes, it did." Generosity of time and resources ensures that we leave a legacy that will outlive ourselves.

Third, play to your strengths. Strengths are not just things at which we excel. They are also things that bring us joy and we can keep improving over a lifetime. I encourage people to use the StrengthsFinder assessment. Figure out not only what you're naturally good at but also what you enjoy so much you'll want to keep doing it your whole lifetime. If you get into the habit of playing to your strengths, others around you will be inspired to play to theirs. Saint Irenaeus said, "The glory of God is man fully alive." When we play to our strengths, we are "fully alive."

Don't fall into the trap of going for success or significance—you can have both. By focusing outward on others' needs, being generous with your time, money, and resources, and playing to your strengths, you will live a life truly worth living.

What's Your Quan?

Do you remember that famous scene in *Jerry Maguire* where Cuba Gooding's character, Rod Tidwell, and Jerry, played by Tom Cruise, are in the locker room? They are having a difficult conversation, and Jerry is trying to convince Rod to drop just a little bit of the attitude and remember why he got into professional sports in the first place. "It wasn't just for the money . . . was it?"

Then again, maybe it was! Earlier in the movie, as Jerry is losing client after client, Rod starts yelling and dancing in exuberance as he says, "Show me the money!" This all happens as Jerry's client list drops to exactly one: Rod Tidwell.

Back in the locker room, Jerry reaches the height of his frustration. After a brief tantrum he begs, "Rod, help me! Help me, help you!"

Rod is eventually able to describe what he is after: "The Quan." It's a made-up word that Rod claims exclusive rights to. He says, "Some dudes might have the coin, but they'll never have the Quan. It means love, respect, community—and the dollars, too! The entire package. The Quan." That's as much of a definition as we get, but this may be the brilliance of the movie because the viewer is invited to define what their Quan is.

So let me ask you: What is your Quan? What are you really going after? What got you into this industry and drove you to become a leader in it? What were you after, and what are you after now?

At first, maybe it was just for the paycheck, for survival. But it likely became more than that, as you began to provide for your family, your team, maybe even gave back to your community. Maybe you realized you had an aptitude for this industry that could likely take you far. Or maybe it was because it's all you've ever known and you wanted to keep a family legacy going.

My Quan didn't change much over the nearly twenty years I was in the auto shop industry. It was always about giving back. Yes, I had to provide for my family, but actually that was the first way I was able to give back. Then the industry allowed me to support causes in the wider community. In the early days we sponsored several nonprofits, from churches to a youth rugby league. Now, through a friend's foundation, our family is deeply involved in orphan care on a global scale. But the thread that ties all this together for me is giving back. As the business has scaled, so did our ability to give back in ever-widening circles.

It's important to ask: What's my Quan?

I did a seminar in 2021 for the FenderBender Management Conference about the five stages of business development that provide the structure for this book. It was an interesting discussion. As we talked through each stage, we discovered that for many of us in the room, freedom means flourishing in all of life.

Yes, financial freedom, where you're rewarded with the dollars for your accumulated knowledge, skill, and risk, is valuable, but what about those higher-order things—love, respect, community—that Rod Tidwell talked about? Are we flourishing in our relationships? Physically, are we healthy or just a bundle of stress and bad habits? Spiritually, do we have a deep sense of meaning and purpose?

I've been asking myself these very questions. I'm in a season where I'm experiencing this freedom. I'm asking the big questions about what it means to flourish in all areas of life, not just the dollars. I'm asking, "What do I really want to do with the remaining years I have on this earth?"

The answers have surprised me. Initially I thought it might be time to get out of this industry. I thought I wanted an escape hatch. Then I thought maybe I should go deeper into it and double down. In the end what I found is that my Quan still holds true: I want to give back. And I want to remove the obstacles in my way that have prevented me from giving back to this industry on a larger scale.

What's your Quan?

Five Lessons from a Monastery Retreat

I went on a retreat in January 2022, shortly after the sale of my businesses. Monasteries have been hosting people for hundreds of years. In Europe they were like the first hotels and intentionally separated by about a day's walk so Christian pilgrims would have a safe place to stay en route to their destination. In fact, hospitality is hardwired into the rules of most monasteries. The monks were to receive guests unconditionally. They were instructed to welcome each guest as if God were visiting the monastery.

For years I had made annual trips to a monastery in Kentucky, and I remembered them with real fondness. All meals were prepared and eaten in silence. Guests were invited to participate in the daily cycle of prayers in the chapel. But it was optional. And I was pretty much left alone to do as I pleased. I typically used these retreats to catch up on sleep and plan the upcoming year. Out of curiosity, I would occasionally pop into one of the prayer times.

But this time I decided to try another monastery. This time I wanted to enter more fully into the monks' schedule of prayers, spending more time in the chapel. I mentioned this to my friend Ralph, who had done several retreats at this particular monastery. I was slightly proud of myself as I announced I may even try to pray on schedule with the monks.

Ralph made it very clear: "Oh you will participate with them. It is expected that if you're there, you enter fully into the life of the monks. You eat what they eat. And pray when they pray. And if you stay more than a couple days, they will put you to work as well."

Surprised, I asked, "Oh, what is their schedule like?"

"Every day they pray from 4:00 a.m. until 7:00 a.m. before breakfast. They eat all meals—mostly vegan by the way—in silence, and there's prayer time before and after each meal. So prayers resume at noon and again at 5:00 p.m. After the dinner meal there is a bit longer final time of prayer as well."

I was doing the math in my head. That's three hours each morning, an hour at each meal plus extended time after the dinner meal. That's about six hours of prayer each day. Oh, and they stand for all prayer times. Whoa! Thankfully they have chairs in the back for guests who may need to sit down. (That'd be me!)

So while this ended up not being exactly what I envisioned, it was definitely what I needed! I want to close this chapter on legacy with the five lessons I took with me from the monastery:

1. *I can do hard things.* In fact, I should! I survived the 4:00 a.m. prayers and the vegan meals. Monasteries are not designed for comfort; they

are designed for meaning. Meaning and comfort aren't always compatible. Staying in a comfort zone never leads to meaning. My goal needs to be living a meaningful, purposeful life. While rest and rejuvenation are needed, seeking constant comfort can be a distraction from a more meaningful life.

2. *My life needs a singular focus.* A monk's purpose is to pray and to seek God in silence and simplicity. I needed to rediscover what my singular focus is in this new season of life. There will always be a draw toward complexity. Choose simplicity.

3. *Humility matters.* For twenty years in this industry, I've been in leadership positions. Everyone on my team wanted my opinion. They needed my direction. They sought my attention. Now, I'm just a guy. And that is a good thing. It doesn't mean I won't lead again in some way. But I have no need to seek it out. And this season feels like a needed break from the spotlight and pressure cooker of leadership.

4. *Don't be in a hurry.* Build habits that lead to incremental change. I used to think about the big leaps of growth. Acquisitions, process breakthroughs, new technology and tools, growth hacks, and shortcuts. Now I'm more interested in the power of repeated incremental actions and daily habits. The Grand Canyon wasn't a breakthrough. Yet look at what a little water over some rocks for a long period of time can do.

5. *Embrace the beauty of austerity.* Monks don't need a lot. Just simple meals. Some prayers that have been prayed for centuries. The same outfit every day. A schedule that doesn't change. What is contentment worth? Learning to be content with little is a big win.

Will I let these lessons resonate in the months and years ahead? I hope so. There is a lot in normal life to distract me. There's the outside forces of technology, the peer pressure of keeping up with others, and the internal drive and ambition to not settle for less. But in the end, a monkish life of simplicity, humility, and deep meaning sounds deeply satisfying.

Conclusion

ARRIVAL AND BEYOND

WE HAVE NOW GONE over the entire framework of all the stages a business goes through.

Starting with the business owner, we discussed the importance of growing our self-awareness, how to take care of ourselves (no one else is going to do it!), and the importance of our character as the foundation on which we build the business.

Next, we looked at the creation stage, that wonderful stage where anything and everything is possible. We are profoundly naive in this stage and have no idea all the things we don't know! But that's okay! This phase is all about dreaming big, living in the imagination where anything is possible, and crafting a compelling vision of what we want our business to be and how it will literally change the world. There is an innocence and an idealism here that are endearing, necessary, and unrealistic. We don't get to live in the ideal for too long, so I encourage you to enjoy it while you can. The wall of chaos is coming soon enough!

Then comes the wall. We start the harrowing journey to learning all the things we don't know. As we begin to discover the hard stuff, we know what we don't know in this phase. And it is scary. It is dark. It is daunting. But it is not insurmountable!

Order needs to be brought from the chaos. A little predictability can go a long way. Predictable sales start to happen when our marketing kicks in.

People start finding us and it's not just a grind of sell, sell, sell. We discover there are good referral partners for us, the people and other businesses that get to our customers before we do. If we do a good job for them and their customers, we start to gain their confidence. The referrals trickle in at first, but eventually we have a flood of customers and a lot of good work waiting for us and our team at all times.

We also start to find some predictability with our teams as we meet regularly with them in a consistent format to check on key measures and celebrate our wins.

Eventually, and I can assure you it feels like forever, we start to gain a sense of control. We start to feel like the flywheel is turning. We start to feel like there is momentum that is not 100 percent dependent on our personal extreme effort. As we move into the control phase, we are looking to build our board of advisors. We're also defining our role as leader and others' roles more clearly. We have processes and standard operating procedures in place for all the core functions of our business. We have checklists that guide our team and guard the quality of our services.

Our customers and, more importantly, our referral partners are taking notice at this point. We're getting accolades, loads of five-star reviews, more referrals, and more consistency in how we deliver our goods and services. We have incentivized employees who get rewarded for a job well done. We are even noticing that some of our team is acting like owners on their best days. There's a pipeline of talent looking forward to working with us if given the opportunity.

Before long we find ourselves slipping into the prosperity phase. We have our right-hand person. We have an executive team that is completely aligned. We have our workers trained and well-resourced to do the work that needs to be done. We've invested in good equipment and tools and world-class training where needed.

This is when we go from owning a job to owning a business to owning an asset. Now we are getting paid better than ever and working less and less. We're also only working in areas of the enterprise that bring us great joy and where we can add unique value. Gone are the days of doing tasks we did well but didn't really enjoy, let alone tasks we neither did well nor enjoyed. We are starting to live in the freedom of a self-sustaining enterprise that throws off good cash flow. We're able to be generous both inside to our team and outside to causes we believe in.

We are starting to face the inevitable questions: Do we sell the business and live off even more passive investments? Do we start the process of transitioning it to our children or the employees? Or do we just let it run and throw off cash requiring little effort from us? This is what people mean when they talk about "you have arrived." This is arrival. You're at the sweet spot now and can make some really fun decisions that all have compelling and interesting outcomes.

The only thing left after this phase is to keep building legacy. Now that you've made it, your attention will turn to your descendants—your kids and those you have mentored. You will be giving generously to causes that mean something to you. You'll be investing in a future that will outlive you—the people and organizations that will carry your values forward.

But remember, we don't wait to start our legacy until the end. We invest in our legacy from the very beginning. From day one our vision should be for more than "to make a lot of money." It's important for us to weave together the strands of our business and our family, our work and our faith, our mental health and our physical health, and so on. Even in the chaos stage, *especially* in the chaos stage, it's important for us to orient to that north star, something way outside of us calling out our best efforts to be patient, do the work, and persevere.

Sometimes it feels like we're in pursuit of something that is a long way off. But as your momentum builds, one day you may be surprised to look up and see it is closer than you ever imagined.

ACKNOWLEDGMENTS

Gary and Karen Rains, for all the training, opportunities and a faith-filled home.

Tracy Rains, for your love. In the words of Nelly, "my lover, my wife, my shawty, my life."

Izaac, **Zoe** and **Tricy** for inspiring me to forgo retirement and relaunch my third act: Legacy.

Greg York, for seeing my potential and believing in my business acumen when I had next to none.

John Jantsch, for helping me make payroll in the early days by being my marketing and sales mentor through your writings.

Dan Sullivan, **Ross Slater**, **Mary Miller** and the Strategic Coach community, for stretching me to go 10x.

John Herman, for implementing EOS into our business and helping us go from chaos to order.

Brandon Schaefer & Cory Carlson, for helping me organize, prioritize, and integrate all Five Capitals.

Chad Allen, for literally taking my words, improving them, and turning them into this book.

Savanah, for helping me get this book across the finish line. Without your help it might still be just a vague hope and a "I almost wrote a book once…"

FREE BONUSES

When you bought this book, you also unlocked a package of bonuses designed to help you thrive as a leader and business owner. These bonuses include a list of recommended books, a retreat guide, and a guide on becoming an authoritative yet gentle leader.

Access them all for free here: **www.rainslegacy.co**

APPENDIX

My Three Biggest Business Mistakes

We all learn from our mistakes. But it's easier, cheaper, and less embarrassing to learn from others' mistakes. The good news for you is that I've made many and I'm going to share my three biggest ones now. For those willing to learn from my mistakes, this is like a cheat sheet for success. It could even save you thousands of dollars and loads of time if you will trust me and treat these like shortcuts to success. So, if I had to start over now, here are three things I would do differently.

Foundations Are Expensive to Fix

First, I would not have scaled so fast. Even though I didn't launch my second location until after twelve years in, I would have waited another couple of years. I wasn't ready for a second location! As soon as I launched shop number two, both shops were destabilized.

My original shop depended on my daily leadership but was now only getting half of my time at best. And the new shop had a full team of very skilled technicians who had just lost their leader and mentor who had been there for decades. In fact, he trained many of them himself from apprentices to A-techs (highly skilled professionals). What ended up happening in the absence of clear processes was I had two businesses running in two different ways. Right about then, another opportunity came along that I didn't want to miss. Rather than unifying the operations, I almost immediately jumped into a third shop.

A better foundation was needed. Clear, documented processes. Unified procedures on everything from how to greet customers to handling inventory to payroll. Instead, I had two shops mostly winging it and then layered the third shop on top of that. There was no symmetry, very little integration, and a shaky foundation. Foundations are complicated and expensive to fix once the building has been erected. It's doable, and we did it. But wow, was it ever hard and came with a big price tag!

I Hired Outside My Industry Too Often

I hired way too many people from outside the industry. I figured if I hired smart and dedicated people—many of whom were my friends—they would learn quickly and all would be well.

I hired smart, dedicated people, and to their credit they learned a lot in a short period of time. However, I didn't account for how much they would have to learn and how long it takes to gain mastery in a particular industry. It wasn't fair to them. I basically threw them in the deep end and said, "Swim!"

Thankfully the friendships in all cases survived and continue to this day. But none of them were able to make it into a long-term career. The lesson for me here was that while friendships are critical to an overall successful life, they should not be the basis for hiring. In retrospect, I was trying to fill my need for friendship through hiring. Big mistake.

The Importance of Having a Visionary *and* Integrator

Lastly, I would have found my right-hand man quicker. I've learned from Gino Wickman, author of *Traction*, that there are two kinds of leaders: visionaries and integrators. I am clearly and unapologetically a visionary. But I needed an integrator.

For the longest time I had a copilot who was a dear friend, but he was also a visionary. That meant we had a lot of ideas and were willing to take risks. We were always ready to grow fast and try new things. Yet we rarely got sustainable traction. Integrators know how to take vision and translate it to the street level. Integrators are able to take all the cloudy ideas of an entrepreneurial organization like ours and make them concrete, understandable, and repeatable.

My final integrator and I were not friends when we started working together. We became friends through our shared mission to improve and scale our organization. Integrators are able to shore up any shaky foundations of the early days. My integrator along with my daughter got all our businesses unified on many important things like our benefits package, a consistent compensation plan, and role descriptions between all the shops.

In writing this, it became clear that my biggest mistakes really relate to one another. And in my final year in the auto repair industry big strides were made to correct these early mistakes and stabilize the whole organization.

Early mistakes can be overcome. We're living proof. It would have been easier if I hadn't made them in the first place, of course. But in retrospect, it came down to some really basic things that allowed us to course-correct: integrated processes and getting the right team members in the right roles.

ABOUT THE AUTHOR

KEVIN RAINS has a rich and varied background that bridges the worlds of ministry and business. With a doctorate in leadership development and a passion for helping others, Kevin spent fifteen years as a pastor before entering the family auto body repair business. Under his leadership, the business grew from $250,000 to over $12 million, expanding from one location to five. Kevin's commitment to integrating faith with professional life has made him a sought-after executive coach and EOS Implementer. He enjoys sharing his journey through writing, speaking, and leading retreats. When he's not working, Kevin loves riding motorcycles and spending time with his wife, Tracy, their three adult children, and two grandchildren.

AS A PROFESSIONAL EOS IMPLEMENTER®, I serve as a teacher, coach, and facilitator. I help entrepreneurial leaders transform their enterprises and, ultimately, their lives.

The Entrepreneurial Operating System® (EOS®) is a comprehensive business operating system that aligns and synchronizes all of the parts of any enterprise. Using a proven process that has been implemented in tens of thousands of companies around the world, I help leadership teams crystallize their vision, gain traction by instilling discipline and accountability, and function as a more healthy and cohesive team.

I love working with small to medium sized businesses that are family owned and mission-minded. Even if you don't live in the Cincinnati area, I can help connect you with an EOS Implementer® close to you. To learn more, visit www.eosworldwide.com/kevin-rains or scan the QR code below.

THE ONE17 FOUNDATION was started in 2016 by Brooke & Aaron Wright. The Rains family are close friends with the Wrights and have supported their mission from the beginning. In 2023, the Wrights asked if they could pass the torch to the Rains family, and we are honored to continue the work of pursuing this vision.

The Rains family has three core values: **Generosity, Hospitality, & Justice**. At the intersection of those three values, we found our mission. This mission, not coincidentally, aligns perfectly with One17.

We plan to give $1,000,000 for children who are abused, under-served, and orphaned around the world by 2030.

As we narrow in on what is most important, we realize there is a gap in the adoption realm. It is lacking education and resources for adoptees, families who adopt, and birth parents. A piece of our mission that ties back to justice is to provide more education and resources and shine a light on the adoptee's voice.

To apply for a grant, make a donation, or access free resources, visit www.one-17.org or scan the QR code below.

NOTES

1. I first read about Saint Anthony and the doctor in Kallistos Ware's book *The Orthodox Way* (Yonkers, NY: St. Vladimir's Seminary Press, 2019).
2. "St. Anthony and the Cobbler," *Tending the Garden of Our Hearts: Meditations for Orthodox Families*, podcast, 8 June 2019, https://www.ancientfaith.com/podcasts/tendingthegarden/st_anthony_and_the_cobbler.
3. Marcel Schwantes, "Warren Buffett Says You Can Spot a Great Leader by Simply Looking for this 1 Trait," inc.com, December 17, 2021, https://www.inc.com/marcel-schwantes/warren-buffett-says-you-can-spot-a-great-leader-by-simply-looking-for-this-1-trait.html.
4. See Catherine Nomura, Julia Waller, and Shannon Waller, *Unique Ability 2.0: Discovery: Define Your Best Self* (The Strategic Coach, 2015).
5. For more information, see the *Wikipedia* article for "Johari window," which contains helpful information as well as some relevant books and articles: https://en.wikipedia.org/wiki/Johari_window.
6. You can learn more about the Five Capitals via Five Capitals Coaching and their free course, https://courses.fivecapitals.net/courses/caffeinate
7. Steven Covey, *The 7 Habits of Highly Effective People* (New York: Simon and Schuster, 2020), 341.
8. See Micheal Hickerson, "Henri Nouwen: What's the Cure for Loneliness?" *Intervarsity Emerging Scholars Network*, https://blog.emergingscholars.org/2012/02/henri-nouwen-whats-the-cure-for-loneliness/.

NOTES

9. I originally heard about this self-coaching model on her podcast: Brooke Castillo, *The Life Coach School*, https://thelifecoachschool.com/podcast/. But there's also a great video about it on YouTube (length: 5:45): https://www.youtube.com/watch?v=gnWfkWaNQuA
10. Jean-Baptiste Say, quoted in "Entrepreneurship," *The Economist*, April 27, 2009, https://www.economist.com/news/2009/04/27/entrepreneurship.
11. Tim Denning, "Elon Musk's Rich Life Is a Friggin Nightmare," Medium.com, March 15, 2022, https://medium.com/illumination/elon-musks-rich-life-is-a-friggin-nightmare-he-tears-up-explaining-it-7b841c49081d.
12. John W. Hogg, *Auto Body Repair and Refinishing* (New York: McGraw-Hill, 1969).
13. John Jantsch, *The Commitment Engine: Making Work Worth It* (New York: Portfolio, 2012).
14. See Nomura, Waller, and Waller, *Unique Ability*.
15. Gino Wickman and Mark C. Winters, Rocket Fuel: *The One Essential Combination That Will Get You More of What You Want from Your Business* (Dallas: BenBella Books, 2016).
16. Chip Heath and Dan Heath, *The Power of Moments: Why Certain Experiences Have Extraordinary Impact* (New York: Simon & Schuster, 2017).
17. Jim Collins, *Good to Great: Why Some Companies Make the Leap... and Others Don't* (New York: HarperBusiness, 2001), 164.
18. Edwin A. Fleishman, Edwin F. Harris, and Harold E. Burtt, *Leadership and Supervision in Industry: An Evaluation of a Supervisory Training Program* (Columbus, Ohio: The Ohio State University, 1955).
19. Charles Duhigg, *The Power of Habit: Why We Do What We Do in Life and Business* (New York: Random House, 2014), chapter 4.
20. Michael Bungay Stanier, *The Coaching Habit: Say Less, Ask More and Change the Way You Lead Forever* (New York: Page Two/Macmillan, 2016), chapter 2.
21. Susan Scott, *Fierce Conversations: Achieving Success at Work and in Life One Conversation at a Time* (New York: Berkley Books, 2004).
22. Will Unwin, "'The Olympic Blues': How Elite Sport Struggles to Cope with the Aftermath," ITV News, 3 August 2021, https://www.itv.com/news/2021-08-03/the-olympic-blues-how-elite-sport-struggles-to-cope-with-the-aftermath.

www.ingramcontent.com/pod-product-compliance
Lightning Source LLC
LaVergne TN
LVHW020430070526
838199LV00025B/586/J